For
Marion

" A Jug of wine
A loaf of Bread
&
Me

And some of that good
New England Cheese

Margaret

In a Glass Lightly

by the same author

SCENES AND CHARACTERS FROM SURTEES
(Edited with Introduction)

FROM ALGIERS TO AUSTRIA: The History of
78 Division in the Second World War

THE PAGEANT OF LONDON

MERRY ENGLAND

REGIMENT OF THE LINE: The Story of
The Lancashire Fusiliers

THE GOURMET'S COMPANION
(Edited with Introduction)

THE COMPLEAT IMBIBER
(Edited annually since 1956)

BEST MURDER STORIES
(Edited with Introduction)

THE WINES OF ITALY

MORTON SHAND'S A BOOK OF FRENCH WINES
(Revised and Edited)

In a Glass Lightly

CYRIL RAY

With illustrations by Quentin Blake

SOUTH BRUNSWICK
NEW YORK: A. S. BARNES AND COMPANY

IN A GLASS LIGHTLY. © 1967 by Cyril Ray.
First American edition published 1969 by
A. S. Barnes and Company, Inc.,
Cranbury, New Jersey 08512

Library of Congress Catalogue Card Number: 75-83493

SBN 498 07459 5

Printed in the United States of America

Contents

To
My fellow-directors,
present and recent,
of the
Directors' Wine Club,
NOBLE FAWCETT
CHARLES HEWETT
GEOFFREY JAMESON, M.W.,
NORMAN NASH
and

DAVID PEPPERCORN, M.W.,
and to our
dear sisters in wine,
the directors of the
Women's Wine Club,
ELIZABETH RAY
JEAN ROBERTSON
and

KATHARINE WHITEHORN,
this book is dedicated . . .

Preface

Some of the chapters in this book quote from, or are based upon, articles of mine that have appeared over the past few years in *The Observer*, *The Spectator*, *The Director*, *Queen* and – to a lesser degree – in various other magazines and periodicals: I am grateful to the respective editors for letting me make use of the material. I am also, and especially, grateful to the distinguished editor of the annual, *The Compleat Imbiber*.

What I have fashioned out of this material makes no claim to being a guide to wine and how to drink it, or buy it, or decant it, or cellar it. There are plenty of such guides, some of which are far more knowledgeable and helpful than any I could write. Some are not.

There are omissions – or what I should have to apologize for as omissions if this little book made any claim to being comprehensive. There is little here about the wines of Italy, for instance, although I have derived much pleasure from them, because I have already written about them at great length elsewhere. I find, too, that I have written much less here about dry than about sweet white wines – rather to my surprise, because I drink relatively little sweet wine and a great deal of dry. Perhaps, although the dry is more interesting to drink, the sweet is more interesting to write about. There is nothing at all about port or sherry or madeira, which are wines that I respect and am interested in, and in which I think I can see, academically, what other people see emotionally, if emotionally is the word, but that I do not care a great deal about, myself. What I see in port is rather what a male homosexual sees in a beautiful and beautifully turned-out young woman. It interests, but it does not stir me.

Nor is this book one of those poetically-written adventures of the soul among masterpieces: I should like to be able to write, but I cannot, as Maurice Healy did of Chambertin, that, "one hears the clang of armour in its depths; Mozart closes his clavecin when it is poured", and so on; or, of Clos de Vougeot, that, "there is a supple firmness about it that suggests Diana . . . it would probably regard Chambertin with the air that Marie Antoinette might have adopted towards Mirabeau."

The late Allan Sichel, one of the greatest tasters the trade has known in recent years, defended, commonsensibly, what other, equally forthright, wine-lovers scoff at nowadays as jargon. "No one should be put off," he wrote in *The Penguin Book of Wines*, which appeared just after his untimely death, "by the flowery and extravagant language sometimes used by enthusiasts. . . . Painters, sculptors and musicians also sometimes express their interpretation of a scene, object or event in a seemingly meaningless and extravagant manner, but no one is prevented by this from enjoying works of art that he understands. . . . The audience may be bored or impressed. The wine will not be affected." And he went on to observe that to describe the 1950 Château Margaux as, "a remarkably pretty girl in a short evening dress," reflected the pleasure of the taster: "it could probably have been described just as accurately as, 'a pretty and attractive wine, but lacking in dignity'. Is there any reason why it should?" (It was another of the trade's great tasters, Mr Harry Waugh, a director of Château Latour and, until recently, of Harveys, who described another year of Margaux, the 1953, as being, "like a pretty girl's bosom: full, firm, sweet and round.")

But it is not in me to let my fancy fly so far, and I admire, but cannot emulate, Mr Warner Allen, classical scholar and historian of wine, who wrote of Malmsey that, "great bottle-age transforms a quintessence of sweetness into a profound magnificence of ambrosial immortality such as the gods of the Golden Age drank on Olympus after they had quenched their thirst in nectar, [it] is perhaps the finest wine in the world." (Mr Warner Allen was once the London editor of the *Yorkshire Post*, and I cherish that sudden access of Yorkshire caution, after all that has gone before, in the word "perhaps".)

It is not merely that I am not that sort of writer: I am not that sort of drinker. Just as for Mr Bernard Levin there are chromatic splendours in Wagner that I cannot comprehend, so these clangs of armour, these ambrosial immortalities, these bottled adumbrations of short frocks and rounded bosoms, alas, elude me. And the analogy between Mr Levin and Wagner on the one hand and me and wine on the other is not far-fetched: Mr Levin has written that, "A Wagner-hangover is much like a liquor-hangover, except that there is no headache; but the ache is transferred to the psyche, whose throbs are much more painful."

I like wine. I enjoy fine wine more than merely good wine, and good wine better than bad or mediocre wine, and my idea of what is fine, what is good, seems much more often than not to agree with the ideas of those who have more knowledge and more experience than I have. But I sometimes suspect that they get more out of the fine and the good than I do – that they have not only more knowledge and more experience, but a greater sensibility – just as there are those who get more out of a great painting or a noble symphony.

Perhaps I was for too long a smoker to be able now to grasp the most elusive subtleties of wine, though I have given up the filthy habit these dozen years and more; perhaps Manchester catarrh has clogged and deadened for too long the passages by which the delicacies of taste and of fragrance should reach the centres of perception. However it may be, I do not have a fine palate – my wife has a finer, as many women have. I do not have that memory for tastes and scents, that capacity for comparing the fragrance and the flavour of today's wine with yesterday's, or even last year's, with which Mrs Pamela Vandyke Price has more than once, in my hearing, confounded experts who have been in the trade since before she was born.

(Mention of these two women prompts me to ask: whence comes the notion that women are less capable than men of appreciating and understanding wine? They ought to be more capable. In this country, at any rate, men seem to be more heavily afflicted with bronchial and respiratory ailments than their wives and daughters, and these are afflictions that diminish the sense of smell – and a sense of smell is of paramount importance in any consideration or appreciation of wine. Women can choose or match a scent or a soap or a toilet-water more promptly and more surely than a man, just as they can taste a sauce in the course of preparing a dinner or say, more decisively than any man not professionally engaged, that this cushion clashes with those curtains, or that such a scarf would never do with such a frock. A sense of smell; a sense of taste; and an eye for colour – most women have all these, and all they lack, to be amateurs of wine, is experience, and this they will never get if they always leave the ordering of wine to their husbands.)

So, having admitted how far I fall short of punditry, all I set out to do here is to comment – not too methodically, I must admit; not too dithyrambically, I hope – on some of the wines I have come across in the past few years, and on what those who know better than I do have taught me about them. On the whole – apart from a few historic champagnes that are now museum pieces – I have concerned myself only with wines that are still obtainable, or that are well within living memory. I find little pleasure, myself, and I think that this is true of others, in reading about wines that I could never have tasted, and never shall. Most of the wines here are still to be enjoyed – which is all that wine is for.

I · *First Faltering Steps*

That much-loved and much-lamented Irish lawyer and wit, Maurice Healy, was a strict teetotaller until he was thirty. By the time he died in 1943, younger than I am now – he was fifty-five – he had become one of the greatest amateurs of wine of recent generations, and had written that most engaging, if extremely mannered, book about its enjoyment, *Stay Me With Flagons*, as well as a knowledgeable monograph on the red wines of Bordeaux.

Perhaps if I had made as late a start as Maurice Healy, I should now be as knowledgeable and as witty. But, alas, I was used to the taste of wine before I was in my teens: my grandparents were sufficiently orthodox to observe the festivals of the Jewish faith with their due ceremony, which meant, with the wines that customarily went with them,

I

and I can still taste, on the palate of my memory, the full, sweet *kosher* wine from Palestine, styled and named after the Spanish Alicante, that even a little boy was allowed to sip on Friday nights and at the Passover.

And yet, although it made this lasting impression, it did not dedicate me then to wine-drinking. The wines that came to England from Palestine in those days were too cloying for anyone to wish to drink as a beverage – or those wines were, at any rate, that were intended for the Jewish market here, specially inspected by the religious authorities, and labelled and sold accordingly. There was no great tradition of wine-drinking except as a ceremony at that time – I do not suppose there is now – among the lower-middle-class Jews from Central Europe, and those who drink wine only occasionally tend to like their wines sweet and rich. (The *sephardim*, who had come originally from Spain and Portugal and Italy were, and are, the heirs to a different culture; had lived longer in England; and were usually richer.)

My immediate family background, in any case, belonged more to the Lancashire of the small cotton-towns than to orthodox Jewry, a world from which my parents had moved one generation and several miles away. When I was a very small boy in Bury, in the First World War, the elementary school I went to, which was run by Wesleyans, had far more influence on my manners, morals, and attitude to strong drink and to the Pope, than had my pious grandparents, who were remote in time, space, culture and, indeed, intelligibility, and whom I saw relatively infrequently. And so, although the taste of wine was not unfamiliar, and the *idea* of wine was accepted – wine thought of as the gift of God, and in which it was proper that God should be honoured – thanks to an already rather remote Jewish past, the connection with which was growing extremely tenuous, there was much, nearer at hand, to militate against

2

one's acquiring a taste for any sort of alcoholic drink. In those days, the respectable folk of a Lancashire town knew beer as the reeking stuff on which the male – and, not infrequently, the female – millfolk, as alien to the small shopkeepers and their wives and children as the Belgian refugees of the time, fuddled themselves until they fell vomiting into the gutters, or fighting each other, with their clogged feet as weapons – "clogging", we called it – when, as the saying went, the pubs "loosed" at ten o'clock.

It was frightening for a child and his mother, returning perhaps from a visit by train to friends in another town (or I should have been in bed long before), to walk in those days through the streets of Bury or Bolton, Oldham or Rochdale, at ten o'clock at night: nobody in this country who has grown up after, say, the nineteen-twenties, or who did not know the industrial North of the time of which I write, can realize how loutishly and terrifyingly drunken so many of his fellow-Englishmen used to be – though I fancy that many Scotsmen still know it of their fellows. Better housing, higher wages and greater security have done more for true temperance than ever the licensing laws did, or will.

Small wonder that at the Clerke Street Wesleyan Day School we were subjected to teetotal lectures (the first school prize I ever won – I must have been about eight or nine – was a certificate for an essay on the evils of alcohol in which I suppose I must have regurgitated, knowing nothing about it myself, the ideas of some Band of Hope lecturer), and it is surprising how strong the Nonconformist-teetotal tradition still is in the North, even in these temperate and enlightened days.

Beer, then, fifty years ago, was beneath our dignity; gin and whisky were beyond our purse; but there was usually a glass of some sweet dessert wine for valued visitors. And a few years after, when the family circumstances had very slightly improved; I was at Manchester Grammar School on a scholarship; and we had moved from Bury to a Manchester suburb (my father's little optician's shop had never done well, and he had found security in a salaried job at the Co-operative Wholesale Society), there was very occasionally a bottle of cheap claret on the sideboard that I found too sour, and that I do not think my father knew a great deal about. (I recall from this period the names St Emilion and St Julien, district wines.) My mother, taken out as a rare treat to Lyons's "State" Café (it was a restaurant, really, but "café" is, or was, the Lancashire word for restaurant) liked to be indulged with a gin-and-It - more, I think, for the sophistication it proclaimed, and for the cherry on a stick, than for the actual taste or effect.

Even when I went up to Oxford, also on a scholarship, I knew nothing about wines, and my modest and unfashionable college was not the one to teach me. Incidentally, I am surprised now, looking back, at how outstandingly good the food was, if not the wines, at the Jesus of those days, let alone at the richer and smarter colleges, compared with the rubbish that is served nowadays even at those colleges that once had a great dining-and-wining tradition. There are still splendid wines to be had at such places, but in most of them the food is beneath contempt. How can a taste and a tradition have been lost so quickly?

Mr Raymond Postgate has recorded, in the very first *Compleat Imbiber*, how - rather before my time, and at St John's - the college Old Ale, "a most remarkable dark beer of great strength," spreadeagled him in the second quad on what was only his twelfth evening as an undergraduate, and pretty well put him off beer for life. What he took to instead was 1878 port, at five-and-sixpence a bottle.

Evelyn Waugh, a little after Mr Postgate's time, a little

4

before mine, and at Hertford, (this was confided to *Compleat Imbiber* 6), was wont to drink a tankard of beer for breakfast. He said he learned – no doubt in the intervals of listening fearfully for "the sound of the English county families baying for broken glass" – to appreciate port, the 1904s being then at their best, and such other dessert wines as Château d'Yquem and Tokay.

For me, though, it was beer that I drank at Oxford: indeed, I drank too much of it, and on it I behaved like what the Russians call a *gooligan*. For it was my pose to be hearty – I played Rugby football; I told dirty stories; and I pinched things, for it was the rollicking thing to do, in those days, somewhere between the General Strike and the Spanish Civil War, for beer-swilling, Rugby-football-playing undergraduates to collect public-house tankards and ashtrays as trophies; municipal and metropolitan red lamps from unguarded holes in the road; and notices requesting one to keep off the grass, not to spit, or please to adjust your dress before leaving.

Forty years on, I look back and wonder what I was like at my work and my play, and have regretfully to record that it was I who, fairly sloshed after a forlorn college cupper against the professionals of B.N.C., which was the St Edmund Hall of my time, made away with a large and heavy wooden notice-board under my voluminous scholar's gown that proclaimed that this was the entrance to the Oxford Society of Women Home Students. The Society has long since become St Anne's College, and I hope that its present undergraduates, then unborn, will forgive it me. Had it not been lost in a wartime change of house, I would return it to them.

What I failed to learn at Oxford, neither schoolmastering nor a spell in a peacetime Royal Air Force officers' mess taught me. The years that the locust has eaten were years in which I

5

drank beer, and it was not until I returned to Manchester, in my late twenties, eventually to become a *Manchester Guardian* reporter, that I began to take wine seriously.

Not, I hasten to add, all that seriously. But I shared a flat with a colleague rather better off and more sophisticated and widely-travelled than I was (he could hardly have been *less* widely travelled: I had never been abroad in my life, and first did so – to Norway, of all improbable places to begin with – when I was twenty-seven), with whom I got into the habit of taking wine with my meals. As did many of my other colleagues and contemporaries, for the *Guardian* was a civilized society – as, I have no doubt, it still is – and few of its members considered that high thinking demanded plain living, though *Manchester Guardian* salaries sometimes necessitated it.* Still, on my five-and-a-half guineas a week, and my flat-mate's seven, we did ourselves rather well, for there was wine to be had in the 1930s at two shillings a bottle, and sometimes we were well enough off to buy it by the case, which brought it down to one-and-tenpence; though this meant, of course, that we drank

---

* C. P. Scott had died only some four or five years before I joined the paper, and Mr Kingsley Martin has recalled his way of life:

"The world in which C. P. Scott lived was very different from anything I ever saw afterwards. His son, Ted, once said to me that his father had always adopted 'the simple principle of finding out what was best and acquiring it'. It was a rich, cultured world, and not at all the ascetic type of life which many people imagined. His must have been one of the few remaining Victorian households of the best upholstered period. The furniture was massive; everything was solid and expensive, designed to last many lifetimes. C.P., as Ted again remarked, never had any notion of equality; he lived in the world of benevolent masters who had no difficulty about getting servants. Once I went to a dinner party at his house. We sat round a great table, loaded with silver plate. There may have been twenty of us. We went in, each with a lady on his arm, and ate many courses of admirably cooked food and drank good wine."

His successor as editor, W. P. Crozier, was obliged to be abstemious for his stomach's sake, like Stafford Cripps, but he understood good living, and A. P. Wadsworth, who followed him, enjoyed good wine.

much more of it, and succumbed to the temptation to ask young women round that we wanted to impress by our worldliness and wealth – perhaps even to soften by wine into malleability – and thus got through it faster still.

The odd thing is that the only wine that I remember individually from those days of thirty years ago (I do not remember the names of many of the young women either, come to that) is one that a Manchester wine-merchant introduced to us as being produced experimentally, and therefore to be had cheaply, he told us, until it had become established – a riesling from the Bordeaux area. It was young and fresh and charming, and it so impressed itself on my memory that for years after the war I asked my friends in the trade – the particular Manchester wine-merchant I had got it from having long gone out of business – where I could find a Bordeaux riesling, only to be told that such a combination was not merely unlikely, which I knew, but quite impossible; that they had never heard of such a wine; and that I must have misremembered.

But I knew I was right, and felt I was on the track of something when, lunching a couple of years ago at a château in the Médoc, I recognized the riesling fragrance and crispness in the white wine grown there, in the claret country, on a very small scale, and was told, yes, they *did* grow a little riesling along with the more usual Bordeaux white-wine grapes, to give a lightness to the wine. But, I was told, I must never quote them by name as doing so: they would lose their *appellation* as "Bordeaux blanc", for the riesling is not officially recognized as contributing to the white Bordeaux. This, of course, because the law-making bodies of a generation or so ago recognized only the "noble" grapes then known and grown in their various regions: the ban on the riesling in Bordeaux was a negative, not a positive one. For in Alsace, as in Germany, it is the noblest of grapes, and I am glad to hear that it is now

7

being permitted in the Bordelais as an admixture – though perhaps only tentatively, and in small proportions. But there is still no Bordeaux riesling, as such, whatever may have been produced experimentally before the war, and I have the feeling that if one were suddenly to appear I might find it as evocative as any *madeleine* in tea. I might even remember the names of some of those girls.

I suppose there must still be some sprigs of rich families who have been brought up from childhood on vintage ports, château-bottled clarets, and the finest of late-gathered hocks, and I wonder if they can possibly know *how* delicious, and in what way, are the wines they have taken for granted. For it is my belief that it was these Manchester flirtations with the cheapest of ordinary wines that laid the foundation of a lasting interest in and appreciation of finer wines – that this was how I learned to take pleasure in the colour of even the commonest red wine, the freshness of a white, the way in which the natural sweetness of a dessert wine will fulfil and round off a meal, and was thus led to distinguish and delight in the subtleties of the finer growths, their even more exquisite fragrance and their almost infinite gradations of flavour, one revealing itself in the mouth after another.

Like most English writers about wine, I owe it to a most scholarly and most hospitable wine-trade that I have had the chance in recent years of making the acquaintance of some of the noblest growths and rarest vintages, many of them at the châteaux or the estates where they are made – tasting one year against another, one vineyard against another, one district against another, which is the only way to *learn* about wines. But I learned to *appreciate* them, however blunderingly, long before, in the Manchester of the 1930s and then in London, in the very first weeks of the war, when I had been sent to the London office before going off to the wars for my paper. I would scour Soho to find a bottle of rough Italian wine at a copper or so cheaper than the one I had bought the other day, and teach myself by adventurous trial and disastrous error why red wine went better with meat than it did with fish; which Italian wines were not only red but fizzy, and came frothing out of the bottle like a mixture of Wincarnis and Eno's; and why a sweet wine from Sicily, say, tasting of muscatel grapes, was not the ideal accompaniment for the chop I had just charred on the minute electric grill of my attic flat.

I do not think that I had then read a single book about wine, and I could have saved myself many a nasty taste in the mouth had I done so, but I was giving myself a grounding, without particularly noticing what I was doing, in some of the basic principles of wine-drinking, and learning to understand not only why one bottle of wine cost five or ten times as much as another, but why it was worth it.

Before I came to such wines, though, there was one more formative experience, and that was Italy. For a time it was Apulia, the heel of Italy, where even in peacetime the wines are indifferent, and southern Italy at the time was cruelly deprived and devastated by war, even beyond its usual state of grinding poverty. But it was still a country where wine was a part of life – we picked the grapes from roadside vineyards to quench our thirst as the Eighth Army clanked and rumbled its way northwards in a cloud of dust – and where men grew wine as a matter of course, and put grimy carafes of it on the table at every meal, equally as a matter of course. And it is salutary for an Englishman to live for a while in a wine-growing country, even – or perhaps particularly – a wine-growing country as simple as Apulia, where wine is neither a symbol by which snobs can demonstrate their wealth or their taste, nor a means of fuddlement, but as natural and as necessary as bread.

9

The deep south of Italy is simple still. Only last year, touring Italy for a book I was writing on Italian wines, I came to Reggio di Calabria, in the toe, and was taken by an official of the wine-growers' association to a local cellar for a tasting. When I asked the cellarman what he called this that he was drawing from the cask, he said, "*vino*," and to my question, "Yes, but what *vino*?" the answer was, "*vino rosso*". He was neither joking nor sulking: he simply thought that I was momentarily at a loss for a common Italian word. Like many of his fellow wine-growers in the south, he would have been hard put to it to give a name to the grapes his wine was made from, and they came from no particular vineyard or commune, but simply from round about.

Naples, though, even in wartime, was another matter; and then for a year in Rome after the war I drank good Italian wines in the company of those who knew much about them. Which is more than I can say of South Africa, visited briefly in 1949 on a mission for UNESCO, where even at good hotels – or what pass in South Africa for good hotels – in the heart of the lovely vineyard country of the Cape, there was never a waiter who could advise between this or that of the often admirably delicate and well-bred wines, and where the white man fuelled his bloody-mindedness on brandy, and denied the black African the consolation even of alcohol.

There was more excuse for the waitresses in the restaurants I frequented during the couple of years I spent in Moscow from 1950 to 1952, for while Moscow is in the latitude of Glasgow and, like Glasgow, is a city of beer-drinkers and spirits-drinkers, the serious wines of the Soviet Union come from the Crimea, which is in the same latitude as Bordeaux, and from Georgia and Armenia, in the same latitude as the toe of Italy. The Georgians and the Armenians are wine-drinkers, but the people of Russia proper – of Muscovy – are not: the waitress at the Ararat, where I used to go for supper after the ballet at the Bolshoi, was a Muscovite herself, even though she served at an Armenian restaurant, and as understandably ignorant of the vintages of the Soviet south as a girl in a Glasgow teashop of the châteaux of the Médoc. I remember, on my first visit, asking for a red table wine to go with the savoury meat patties I had ordered, and the girl brought me one sweet, port-like wine after another, as fast as I could taste and reject them. At last, I had sipped my sickly way through the list until I came to a big, hearty Georgian wine that I smacked my lips over, something like the wines of the Rhône or of northern Italy, only to hear the waitress say – in so far as I understood her Russian, though her gestures were expressive: "I didn't think you'd like *that*. That's what *I'd* call sour."

There are some respectable Soviet table wines; the difficulty is to track them down through the mazes of a wine-list composed of unfamiliar names printed in unfamiliar characters, with little help, unless one is in the south, from waiter or waitress. Even in the south there is not the knowledge of the vintages of western Europe that would enable a wine-waiter to explain a wine by comparison or analogy. I found eventually that two wines from Georgia, the white Tsinandali and the red Moukouzani, were pleasantly palatable, and I had to be left un-called as an expert witness in the "Spanish champagne" case (in which the champagne-shippers successfully defended their exclusive right to the name "champagne" against the shippers of Perelada), although I had been invited to give evidence on behalf of the champagne houses, and had accepted the invita-tion because in a playful article in *The Director* I had written of these two wines that, "it would have been easier had they been called (say) Soviet Chablis and Soviet claret, which would have given me an idea of their general *type*, without at all deceiving me into thinking that they were French, and would have obviated my having to wade through all sorts of dessert wines that could well have been called Soviet port or Soviet old brown sherry."

All my sympathies were, and are, with the champagne-shippers: words should have a precise meaning, and in this country far too many beverages and foodstuffs sail under mis-leading colours. But my plea for special treatment of a special case (and "Tsinandali", whether spelled in Cyrillic or in the Persian-like Georgian characters – in the Soviet Union the label has it in both, but nothing in Roman lettering – seemed to me a very special case indeed) would have been a dangerous weapon in the hands of counsel for Perelada.

So I was denied the pleasure of an appearance in court when M. André Simon (I was told later), on being led by plaintiffs' counsel to agree that he was an acknowledged authority on food and drink, said, "Sir, I am full of my subject"; and Mr Raymond Postgate, to whom Perelada's counsel had said, challengingly, "In other words, Mr Postgate, *you* want to reserve the word 'champagne' only for the most expensive kinds of champagne, so that only the *rich* can enjoy cham-pagne," devastatingly replied, "What *your* clients want to do is to call margarine butter, so that the poor can enjoy butter."

This was in 1960, by which time I had somehow become well-enough established as a writer about wine to be con-sidered as an expert witness, though I still do not quite know how, and though I knew perfectly well that I was far from being truly expert. In ten years on *The Sunday Times* up to my resignation in 1956 I had written only once about wine, and then rather indirectly – a light-hearted account of a visit to the Rhineland – and although I had been invited in 1953 or there-abouts to contribute to *The Compleat Imbiber*, at that time a paper-backed magazine that Gilbeys sent to their friends and customers, it was because Mr Jasper Grinling, who was then Gilbeys' youngest director, responsible for publicity and packaging, had liked my pieces of descriptive reporting in *The Sunday Times* – not because he had any reason to suppose that I knew, or even cared, anything about wine.

But in 1956, to celebrate the firm's centenary, it was decided to publish a bound volume of selections from the magazine, and I was asked to edit the new book, which then became an annual (it is now sponsored by Harveys). At about the same time, a former *Sunday Times* colleague, Mrs Muriel Forbes, who had become woman's page editor of *The Times*, invited me to contribute a monthly article to her page – the first articles on wine that it had published – which did nothing to make me known to my readers, for in those dignified days contributors to *The Times* were anonymous, but did serve to widen my circle of acquaintance among members of the trade, whose advice I sought. I also began at about the same time to write occasional notes on wine for *The Spectator*, the staff of which I joined in 1958, as foreign editor, diplomatic correspondent and assistant editor, but soon with a regular corner for my "Wine of the Week". In the same year I began my regular articles on wine in *The Director* and in *The Observer* – first of all as an outside contributor, though I eventually joined the staff of *The Observer* in 1962, when the proprietor of *The Spectator* became a Tory candidate, and I resigned.

One of the glossy magazines had already introduced an article of mine in 1957 with the statement that I was an "authority on wine". But I was not, and I am not. The true authorities on wine are to be found among those members of the trade who have been tasting wine for a living all their lives, and whose livelihoods depend not on knowing that this fine wine is more agreeable than that, but on knowing why and, more important still, on being able to taste the young wines from the cask that to me still taste like sucking a brass rail, and knowing what they will be like in how many years' time. A journalist's job is to know who the experts are, to consult the right expert at the right time, to get the facts right, and to make them readable.

Of course, a man would be a fool who, having enjoyed for ten years or so the company of experts, and the opportunity of drinking under their tutelage the finest wines, rare old wines, and young wines, did not learn a good deal. And there are a very few journalists and other writers who, unlike me, can be counted as experts in their own right: M. André Simon (but he has had many years in the trade himself), Mr Raymond Postgate, Mr Edmund Penning-Rowsell, Colonel Andrew Graham and Mrs Pamela Vandyke Price. Of the new generation, young Mr Hugh Johnson and young Mr Julian Jeffs lack nothing in taste and discrimination. I have learned much from these friends and colleagues, but the great judges of our time are in the British wine trade, and even the distinguished writers I have named would join me in acknowledging them as our masters.

A couple of years ago, in a *New Statesman* review of *Compleat Imbiber 6*, Mr Francis Hope (a socialist, like myself, as I discovered in the course of subsequent correspondence, in which he wrote that, "there is no logical inconsistency between voting Labour and being greedy: I do one and am the other"), wrote that, "the politics of food and drink are always difficult. I intellectually assent to the arguments and example of socialist experts (Postgate, Ray), but nurse, at the back of my mind, a conviction that if a man starts talking about the glories of Lafite '34 he is unlikely to support the reintroduction of super-tax. All reason is against it, all belief is for it." And he went on to quote that reactionary bully, George Saintsbury, whose "pages are filled with scornful footnotes denouncing Pussyfeet and Radicals as if they were the same miserable thing." But then Saintsbury was rather in favour of shooting conscientious objectors and coalminers on strike, and I do not see why talking about the glories of Lafite '34 should mark one as a reactionary any more than would talking about the glories of the Sistine Chapel, or the merits of Mozart.

It is true that there has always been a puritanical, hair-shirt element in British radicalism, though I think that it belongs to the past, and that it is dwindling both in support and in importance. But there are also those who believe that what socialism is about is, as Mr Postgate has written, "a freer and better life for the people as a whole". This in the course of an article he wrote, at my invitation, for *The Compleat Imbiber*, about "Saint Cobden and Saint Cripps", the two statesmen, both of the Left, "to whom sensible wine-drinkers owe most". (Cobden's commercial treaty with France in 1860 reduced the duty on French table wines from 12s. to 2s. a dozen bottles; Cripps, in 1945, halved the duty on all table wines.)

There is not enough of the finest of anything to go round, and it is monstrous that what there is should go only to rich vulgarians, like the British big-business man I met at a French hotel, with his sulky daughter and his golden-curled, trousered and high-heeled wife, who drank Mouton-Rothschild 1953, at about £7 a bottle, at every lunch and every dinner, washing each bottle down with Coca-Cola ("red wine makes you so thirsty, o'boy"). He always bought Mouton-Rothschild, he told me, because he knew the name and reckoned it was a sound one. He would have been just as happy with Mouton Cadet, and serve him right.

There is an obligation on those who care about good wine – as there is on those who care about music or painting or any other civilized pleasure – to defend standards against the mass-producers, the takeover-bidders, the advertisement copywriters, and the public-relations smart-alecks, who make their quick bucks and their gossip-column reputations out of the cheap, the slick and the shoddy. There are politicians, I hope, who regard it as their job to make it possible for more and more of what used to be called the workers, and of what are still the under-privileged, to afford the time and the money to enjoy the good things of life. It is the job of journalists and critics, as well as of creative artists, to see that there is a good life left for them to enjoy.

True, there is not enough Mouton-Rothschild 1953 for everyone in the world to drink, but not everyone in the world would ever want to drink it – some would genuinely prefer Coca-Cola, or a sweet wine, or a television set, or a rare postage stamp, or a new suit. What is important is that it should be there; that everyone capable of appreciating it should have an equal opportunity of getting it, and in the meantime that those people should not be cheated and imposed upon who have not yet had the chance of developing their taste and their critical judgment. Only the best (of its kind) is good enough – not for the rich, but for everyone. And maintaining the standards of the very best has its effect on the more modest. The horse-power and the braking efficiency of a Rolls-Royce are important, not only to the rich businessman who uses it, but because one cannot ignore or abandon Rolls-Royce standards and still expect good workmanship of its kind in a Morris or an Austin. The *bourgeois* growths of the Médoc are as good as they are – which is very good indeed – because of the standards set by Lafite and Latour, Margaux and Mouton. One reason why a French lorry-driver eats well is that so does the rich Parisian.

What goes into the belly of a human being should be decently made and honestly described, whether it is for a tycoon or a typist. The rich reactionary who wants to afford the best for himself by selling rubbish to the poor is a knave.

16

The idealist of the Left may be as insensitive to wine as I am to music, and small blame to him – only pity – but if he thinks that because he does not mind what he eats and drinks neither should anyone else, he is a fool. There is no more virtue in not minding what you eat and drink than in not minding whom you go to bed with.

2 · *Short Ones*

Not long ago, according to a Moscow newspaper quoted here in the trade press, one Comrade Popov brought down a Soviet crop-spraying aeroplane with an empty vodka bottle. Comrade Popov, an official of the Communist Party of the Soviet Union, was enjoying a picnic, when the low-flying machine sprayed chemical powder into his bowl of soup. Pausing only to drain the contents of the bottle, Comrade Popov hurled it at the aircraft (crying out variants on his own name, no doubt, as he did so), hit the wing, and caused the pilot to make a forced landing. "Didn't know what had hit him," is probably a fair summing-up of the pilot's feelings.

As a result of a Moscow newspaper agitation, Comrade Popov, who had at first been only mildly reprimanded, was actually expelled from the Party, but whether for the damage he had caused to the aeroplane and the pilot's professional pride, or for scoffing a whole bottle of vodka at a time when the bigwigs in the Kremlin were counselling the citizenry that it is more *kulturny* to drink Georgian and Armenian wines, I do not know. My own view is that the title of Hero of Soviet Labour or Master of Sport of the Soviet Union has been bestowed on persons less quick-thinking and less gifted than one who, full of vodka, can hit even a low, slow aeroplane in flight with the bottle he has just emptied.

No doubt it will add to the strange Western legend about vodka and its potency, according to which British, French and American officers, inured to pink gins, Pernods and ten-to-one martinis, used to fall stupefied under the table when plied with vodka by their Soviet comrades-in-arms in that brief period of allied mateyness just after the war. It was the legend rather than the liquor that did the trick, and the legend is far older than the Second World War: Russia, in the eyes of the West, has always been a mysterious place, whether under the Czars or under the commissars, and so vodka has always been credited with a mysterious potency.

George Saintsbury maintained, and it was not the only silly thing he wrote, that the Russian Revolution was brought about largely by the Czar's banning of vodka, as a wartime measure, and that the Revolution was as fierce as it was because the revolutionaries made up for lost drinking-time. But there are footnotes about it in the Russian history books: Peter the Great, writing to his wife from Paris, complained, "There is only one bottle of vodka left: I don't know what to do."

Vodka is not really mysterious at all. Its name means nothing more than "little water", and it is a simple spirit that has been distilled in Russia, Poland and Finland since time immemorial, from rye or maize or – rarely – from potatoes, but best of all from wheat, in much the same way as Scotch grain whisky is made, but with more rectifying and filtering, so that a virtually tasteless spirit results. It is the same sort of thing as schnapps or akvavit, though these are flavoured; it has the same sort of strength, as a rule, and the Russians drink it in the same sort of way: well-chilled, tossed off neat at a gulp from a very small glass, or silver jigger, and with salty, fishy, greasy *zakouski*, which are hors-d'œuvre, such as caviar and salt herring.

I refer to it as Russian, not as Soviet, for vodka came originally from Russia proper, unlike the wines of the Union, which come from the southern constituent republics, chiefly Georgia, Armenia and the Ukraine, and which it is as wrong to call "Russian" as it would be to speak of "English whisky" – they are Soviet, but not Russian, just as Scotch whisky and Irish whiskey are British but not English. Now its use has spread all over the Union, just as whisky has spread all over the United Kingdom, and yet, common as it is, there is still a ceremonial about the way in which it is served. In the better restaurants there are heavily cut little glasses for it, the size of liqueur glasses, sometimes with clear cutting through coloured glass, like the old fashioned hock glasses, or Baccarat overlay paperweights. And every fancy shop in Moscow and Leningrad sells pretty little vodka cups in coloured enamel on silver-gilt, or in silver deeply engraved, like the back of a Victorian watch.

In spite of the legend, vodka need be no stronger than gin or whisky, and in this country it rarely is: of the British-made brands, the more popular of the two Smirnoff varieties is 65 degrees, and Relska 65·5 – standard gins and whiskies are 70 degrees, the same as the standard Stolichnaya vodka that we import from the Soviet Union. Though there are stronger vodkas to be had here, of course, most of them Polish. Indeed, there is a Polish top-of-the-head remover, recommended only to serious students, called Pure Polish Spirit, 140 degrees proof – absolute alcohol being 175·1 – of which it was once observed that it was the cheapest and handiest method, since the virtual disappearance of the French Foreign Legion of legend, of not remembering whatever it was that chaps used to go to Sidi-bel-Abbes to forget. And there is a Polish Vodka Starka, which is made from rye and not, like most Russian vodka, from wheat, aged in cask to a pale straw colour and a slight tang of sherry, that reaches a formidable 87 degrees. What the Poles are particularly good at, though, is producing flavoured vodkas on a commercial scale, whereas the Russians drink theirs unflavoured, or flavour their own at home by steeping herbs or fruit or lemon-peel and the like in the local flavourless vodka. Easily obtainable now in this country, and at the normal 70 degrees, are Vodka Jarzebiak, slightly tinted by, and flavoured by rowan berries, and the best-known of all Polish vodas, Vodka Zubrowka, the palest possible green in shade from the zubrowka grass that gives it its fresh, clean herby taste.

Such vodkas make strong, but not too strong, eye-openers to toss back, ice-cold, before a meal, or with hors d'œuvre, just as the Russians drink their own unflavoured vodkas with caviar. There is much to be said, and especially on a cold evening, for serving well-chilled vodka neat, in tiny glasses, with smoked salmon or potted shrimps. But our own way with vodka is based on that of the Americans – from whom, not from the Russians, we have taken the vodka-drinking habit (and I think that the Americans took to it, which they did at the worst period of the cold war, rather on the savage's principle of drinking the blood of the brave enemy, so as to absorb his strength and his courage).

Like the Americans, we use vodka not neat but as a mixer, for which it is ideally suited: tasteless, colourless, odourless, it gives strength and kick to other liquors, from tomato juice to vermouth, without affecting look, smell or flavour. Or, come to that, affecting look or smell of the consumer: "it leaves you breathless," was the Smirnoff slogan in American advertisements, but the Americans had already decided that the prime virtue of vodka was that you could get stinking and not stink.

There are those who have taken to vodka and tinned tomato juice, as being not so fierce as the vodka neat, and others who approve of it as being not so slimy as the lurid juice. But I am not much of a one myself for what I can only describe as the Perfectly Bloody Mary; nor for bitter lemon, which is also laced with vodka these days; and I would rather have champagne than vodka in my orange juice, so I am no expert on what is called in the United States a "screwdriver" – perhaps by some analogy with the "gimlet", – which is erroneously believed to consist of gin and orange juice.

But I am whole-heartedly in favour of vodka with vermouth, for not only has it no marked taste of its own to quarrel with those of the herbs in the vermouth, but vodka seems actually to intensify rather than to diminish the vermouth's flavour. Indeed, I am told that there is scientific support for this belief: the straight unflavoured alcohol vaporizes and carries the scents (and, therefore, the tastes) of the herbs into the nasal passages. At home, I use a light, dry Chambéry vermouth and one of its sweeter cousins – either Nivolet or Dolin's Chambéryzette, which are the same vermouth, flavoured with wild strawberries. Either I drink them straight, very cold, or with whatever proportion of vodka I feel that the trials, tribulations and telephone-calls of the working day have entitled me to – I find half-and-half of vodka and strawberry vermouth an admirable pick-me-up and appetizer. By the same token, there seems much to be said for making a version of the classic martini with vodka as an alternative to gin – it is slightly different in flavour, but equally good. It is not, strictly speaking, a true martini, but I cannot bring myself to call it a vodkatini.

But there has been an enormous change since the war in our before-dinner drinking habits, of which the present popularity of vodka is only a part. In 1964, on the eve of his ninetieth birthday, Somerset Maugham, being interviewed by Mr Stephen Coulter, the distinguished Paris correspondent of the *Sunday Times*, broke off for a moment from his reminiscences to say, "Suppose we had a cocktail . . .", and the interviewer, who had been observing how up-to-date was Mr Maugham's manner and vocabulary, put the words, "a cocktail", into quotation marks and added, in brackets, "it was his only dated term". Reading the interview, I felt dated myself to see "cocktail" so described. Could it, I wondered, really be as old hat as all that?

Certainly, all those mixed-up drinks for the mixed-up drinkers of the 1920s, when Somerset Maugham was no older than I am now – "Monkey Gland" and "Mah Jongg" among them: "Between the Sheets" and "Bosom Caresser"; "Wembley" and "White Cargo" and even, heaven preserve us, the "League of Nations" cocktail – have gone the way of those named after the stars of the silent films of the time: Mary Pickford and Douglas Fairbanks, Will Rogers and the Gish Sisters. Yet I still find myself invited to what the cards describe as "cocktail parties", even if what I am offered at them is sherry or champagne, and I am sure that the word "cocktail" must still be current usage to describe those that are shaken (or, more probably these days, stirred) and served in what hotels still refer to as their "cocktail bars", though in those of the smartest Paris hotels the most sophisticated habitués now drink Scotch whisky.

"Cocktail" seems to be a very generic term now, applied only to a bar or a party. It must be a very long time since I was offered any mixed drink (any short mixed drink, that is: I exclude gin-and-tonic, or brandy-and-ginger ale) in a

23

private house other than a martini – which is what, in fact, Somerset Maugham's companion-secretary set about mixing for Mr Maugham and his interviewer – a Daïquiri (and that only in New York) or a champagne-cocktail. And I think that even when a martini or a Daïquiri is offered it is by name, never in terms of, "would you like a cocktail?"

It is odd to think that it was largely the Americans who brought about and popularized the great cocktail cult of between the wars, with the need for all that paraphernalia, all that measuring, all that shaking – the Americans, who are supposed to be all for speed, streamlining and efficiency – whereas a glass of sherry or of champagne rather than a cocktail before dinner saves time, trouble and energy, and is much more a custom of what is regarded as the leisurely old world.

But perhaps American admiration was extended to the cocktail not for speed in the making but for speed in the results. As Ogden Nash sang, of breaking the ice:

> Candy
> Is dandy,
> But liquor
> Is quicker.

Now, there are far fewer cocktails being mixed than in those far-off days of cloche hats and Carpentier, of Bright Young Things and the Charleston, and even the very word, dropped in 1964 from the lips of a nonagenarian, strikes a middle-aged journalist on a sober Sunday newspaper as being *démodé*. Yet the word has had a longer run than the thing itself, which took far longer to establish itself in England than most American innovations. Although, as Mr James Laver has observed, both the word and the drink were known to the "fast set" of the Edwardian era, and in the novels of E. Phillips Oppenheim, they made no impact on ordinary middle-class people, or on the popular press, until after the

First World War, and Mr Alec Waugh has written that, "the idea came, presumably, from America. By 1927 it was already established in London. There are indications that during 1925 it was finding itself. Guests were tending to drop in for a cocktail at six, rather than for 'a dish of tea' at half-past four; but in 1924 it was relatively unknown. The present writer recalls how, in April 1924, he discussed with C. R. W. Nevinson, the painter, and his wife, the difficulty of finding anything to do in London in the winter between tea and dinner. The Nevinsons decided that it might be a good time at which to give a party and sent out an announcement that they were emerging from their winter retirement and would be at home on the last Saturday in April between five and seven.

"Questioned, years afterwards, they were vague as to the number of invitations they sent out; but some thirty glasses were arranged beside a large earthenware jug containing a yellow, coolish but not cold mixture, in which rum was the chief ingredient. Only two guests arrived. The Londoners of the Nevinsons' acquaintance – and the Nevinsons touched life at very many points – were puzzled by the novelty of the invitation. And Londoners tend socially to avoid what puzzles them.

"Remembering the experience of the Nevinsons, this writer, wishing to give a cocktail party in October 1925, took the precaution of inviting his friends to tea at half-past four and not starting to serve cocktails until half-past five. He served a rum swizzle, mixed by a New York friend. It was sweet, cold and strong, and a distinguished woman novelist who, because it was cold and sweet, mistook it for a kind of sherbet, failed to achieve her subsequent engagement for dinner. Within a mere eighteen months the cocktail party was an established form of entertainment."

Yet it is much longer ago than the paintings of C. R. W.

Nevinson, or even than the novels of E. Phillips Oppenheim, that London first came across the cocktail, both name and concoction – though London has forgotten. I did not, myself, realize how long ago it is until I came across a copy of *How to Mix Drinks, or the Bon-Vivant's Companion*, published in New York in 1862, no doubt to help in bolstering Yankee morale after Bull Run, and written by Jerry Thomas, described on the title-page as, "Formerly principal Bar-tender at the Metropolitan Hotel, New York, and the Planter's House, St. Louis". The contents include a list of cocktails, referred to as such, and the anonymous writer of the preface to Jerry Thomas's book records what may have been the first acquaintance of the British public with the word and with the drink:

"We very well remember", he writes, "seeing one day in London, in the rear of the Bank of England, a small drinking saloon that had been set up by a peripatetic American, at the door of which was placed a board covered with the unique titles of the American mixed drinks supposed to be prepared within that limited establishment. The 'Connecticut eye-openers' and 'Alabama fog-cutters', together with the 'lightning smashes' and the 'thunderbolt cocktails', created a profound sensation in the crowd assembled to peruse the Nectarian bill of fare, if they did not produce custom."

I can well imagine the "profound sensation" experienced by a top-hatted, frock-coated, early Victorian City gent at being invited to partake, in the very shadow of the Bank of England, of a Connecticut eye-opener or a thunderbolt cocktail: all that surprises me is that his astonishment does not reverberate through the pages of Victorian literature – in Thackeray, or Dickens or Surtees. I do not know that the drink or the word for it occurs in a single one of their novels, though I see from the dictionary that Thackeray calls a stuck-up fellow a "cocktail", as one might say a coxcomb.

Curiously enough, there is no recipe in the book for any of the drinks offered at the saloon behind the Bank, but there are some others that must have been equally dynamic. I especially liked the learned author's comment on his own Punch Jelly, the recipe for which is too long, alas, to give here, and I think that it would be too complicated, anyway, for present-day concocting:

"a very agreeable refreshment on a cold night, but should be used in moderation; the strength of the punch is so artfully concealed by its admixture with the gelatine, that many persons, particularly of the softer sex, have been tempted to partake so plentifully of it as to render them somewhat unfit for waltzing or quadrilling after supper."

Of the lineal descendants of the Alabama fog-cutters of a hundred years ago, and of the Bosom Caressers of forty, only the martini seems to have survived and to be likely to go on surviving. (I write of my own country: when I was last in New York, it was closely rivalled there by the Daïquiri, but of that more later.) In the United States, the martini has become so much what we now call a status symbol – a means of displaying expertise (by those, for instance, who put in, not an olive but a small artichoke heart, or six dill seeds); a proclamation of virility (ten of gin to one of vermouth, and make the gin vodka, anyway); and a testimony to wealth (solid gold martini pitcher) that the object of the exercise has been somewhat lost sight of.

This explains some of the recipes I once read in an article in an American magazine, entitled "172 Ways to Make a Martini" – recipe No. 13 advised, "keeping the vermouth in a separate room and bringing it to within three feet of the gin bottle at cocktail hour". I think the compiler of the 172 recipes cheated a little, for recipe No. 10 is gin to vermouth in the proportion of 3·7 to one, and recipe No. 11 is 3·8 to one.

The author's own preference was for five of gin to one of vermouth, but he admitted, implicitly, to being something less than the all-American husky male, as the majority of his compatriots, he said, preferred 7·5 to one. In Ernest Hemingway's *Across the River and into the Trees*, the American colonel who is the central figure and, I suppose, a sort of deutero-Hemingway, calls for, "Two very dry martinis. Montgomerys. Fifteen to one ..." – sneering at a better soldier than himself who had resolved that no army under his command should suffer the losses that the British had suffered in World War One, and that the United States Army had not. Having seen them for himself, as Hemingway had not. The said martinis were served to the colonel in Harry's Bar in Venice, the right sort of place for that sort of drink – and that sort of American.

And yet Americans have complimented me on the strength of my martinis – two to one, but with no ice in the mixer or the glass, and the driest possible French vermouth. The secret is to keep gin and vermouth in a very cold refrigerator, and to mix the martini in, and serve it from one of those German jugs, or Italian carafes, with a separate ice-container. My view is that a martini should *taste* of something – and that is why there must be some vermouth; it should buck one up after a day's work, hence the gin; and it must awaken and refresh the palate for the dinner to come, not deaden it – and that is why there should not be too much gin, or too many helpings.

I was glad to have confirmation of this view when I sought instruction from an expert. A martini cocktail need not be made with Martini vermouth: it takes its name from a barman of many years ago in the New York Waldorf-Astoria whose invention it was, and whose name, I believe, was Martinez. The drink became a martini by natural confusion with the vermouth – and what a stroke of luck for the firm! All the same, it seemed appropriate to sit at the feet of the veteran barman of the firm of Martini and Rossi, at the bar of their Martini Terrace that overlooks Trafalgar Square from the sixteenth floor of New Zealand House. (Although I do not use Martini vermouth myself: I use a pale, light vermouth de Chambéry, of which more later.)

In his trim white coat, and with his spectacles and rather precise manner, Jimmy the barman looked as though he might be a scientist in a laboratory; in fact, he had been in turn a waiter and then a barman for fifty years, for forty of which he presided over the American Bar of the old Carlton Hotel, on the very site where he now mixes martini cocktails with Martini vermouth on the Martini Terrace for the house of Martini.

Jimmy chose the more dry of the two Booth's gins, which is the colourless "High and Dry", along with the driest of the three Martini vermouths – the other two being dark and the "bianco", both sweet. Nowadays in this country when you ask for a martini, the experienced barman mixes a *dry* martini, as Jimmy did – two of gin, one of vermouth, poured over broken ice and stirred (not shaken) before being poured immediately into a glass (not long enough on the ice to be seriously diluted). But I forget the third ingredient. Over my martini Jimmy held a sliver of lemon peel, giving it a deft twist so that the oil sprayed into the glass before dropping it in. He then demonstrated over the back of my hand what an appreciable amount of the essential oil came out of so small a twist of peel, and how necessary that the lemon be ripe and the peel soft.

Normally, I am not much of a martini drinker: before a meal, I usually prefer my vermouth straight, or a glass of cool white wine or, if lucky, a glass of champagne. But I had just arrived in London after a tiring journey from the country, and I welcomed the slightly greater kick of my dry martini. Now, though, allowing myself one more drink before lunch, I wanted something a little less strong and I asked Jimmy for the classic martini – half-and-half gin and vermouth. Not that the difference in strength is all that great, for the vermouth is around 30 degrees proof to the gin's 70 degrees, and the total difference in alcoholic content between the martini and the dry martini can only be about 3 per cent. But the half-and-half seems appreciably blander, with more flavour and less strength, and I felt that I had hit on an admirable progression of drinks for before lunch after a tiring morning – first the sharp dig in the ribs of the dry martini, and then the gentler pat on the back of the classic half-and-half.

And I was glad to see that Jimmy agreed with me about the fearsomeness of such American concoctions as seven-to-one and ten-to-one, and of the barbarity of that keeping the vermouth and the gin in separate rooms. It seems to me that if one wants strength and flavour, in that order of importance, then the dry martini is the thing. Given that the gin and the vermouth are of good quality, as these unquestionably were; that the mixture is *not too long on the ice*; and that there is *no ice in the glass*, this is strong enough for even very serious drinkers. (At home, my martinis are stronger than Jimmy's by the very tiniest margin: I use the same proportions, but *no ice at all*, simply, as I have explained, keeping both gin and vermouth bottles in a very cold refrigerator.) And if, on the other hand, one wants flavour and strength, in *that* order, then equal parts of gin and vermouth will give it, and still without any serious loss of alcoholic strength. People who like vermouth so little that they want hardly any in their martinis might well do better with that excellent reviver, the pink gin.

I downed my second drink, and set off for lunch. It had

been an agreeable interlude and an interesting discussion: it was only as I left the bar that it occurred to me to ask Jimmy what *his* favourite drink was. "Scotch and water," said Jimmy.

In the Royal Air Force as I knew it, more than thirty years ago, there was still a strong naval tradition, and both the commanding officer and adjutant of the station on which I served the longest had both been first in the Royal Navy and then, during the First World War, in the Royal Naval Air Service. So I have drunk many a pink gin in my time, and still do, occasionally, at the hospitable house of my near neighbour, George Hardinge, now a publisher, but once a sailor, whose pink gins must be the most potent ever served ashore.

There are those – sailors especially and, naturally enough, the distillers of Plymouth gin – who insist that pink gin should always be made with Plymouth gin, never with London. Equally naturally, the distillers of London gin insist otherwise. Plymouth gin is not, as is popularly supposed, sweeter than London, but it is more pungent. I have never been able to understand how George Saintsbury could have thought it, "more delicate in flavour": M. André Simon gets it right in his *Concise Encyclopaedia of Gastronomy*: "a distinctive type of Gin, heavier and richer than *London Gin*, unsweetened, and the nearest approach to *Hollands Gin* distilled in England." When I drank pink gins at Gordon's distillery in Islington, the chairman claimed that the lighter flavour of his gin, for instance, let the bitter tang of Angostura in a pink gin come through more clearly than does the fuller Plymouth. Made with either type of gin, the drink is an appetizing one, but made with Plymouth it tastes more of gin, with London more of bitters.

There seems to be no classic recipe for a pink gin, as there is (in spite of the heretical American deviations) for a dry martini. The *Savoy Cocktail Book* counsels one dash of Angostura to two ounces of gin and allows nothing else – not even ice or water. The American Mr David Embury's *Fine Art of Mixing Drinks* goes in for strips of lemon peel and even a few dashes of curaçao, which would horrify many a sailor of my acquaintance. There is no question, though, but that the bitters must be Angostura, that remarkable invention of a Waterloo veteran who went adventuring with Bolivar in the 1820s, with its enchantingly old-fashioned wrapper-cum-label, bearing its long messages in four languages and impossibly small print. And if anyone wonders why Angostura is so cheap in the United States and so damnably dear here it is because the Americans in their wisdom class it as flavouring matter, on which the duty is negligible, whereas we, in our folly, treat it as spirit, and tax it to the uttermost. And the gospel according to the head of Gordon's is two or, at the most, three drops of this precious liquid on a couple of small cubes of ice and a double measure of gin, diluted if desired with up to half as much water.

This is how we drank it at the distillery, and a dry, clean concoction I found it, with not so much bitters as to drown the taste of the gin, not so much taste of the juniper and coriander, with which gin is flavoured, as to prevent the tang of the bitters coming through. Pink gin is not so widely drunk as it used to be: it has always been an east-of-Suez empire-builder's drink, and naval officers have drunk it where ratings have drunk rum. Now there are not so many empire-builders east of Suez – not building *our* empire, anyway. Not so many N.O.s, either, and more drinks competing for their attention – the lighter rums among them. But it seems to me as good an aperitif as most, and one that ought to be more popular than it is, for it fits in with the current taste for dry, light, bitter drinks – there is nothing sweet or cloying about a pink gin.

Especially, I am surprised that the Americans have not taken to it, in their passion for drinks dry and things British, such as J. and B. and Cutty Sark whiskies, for gins-and-tonics and Dunhill pipes and Burberry coats and Bermuda shorts. I am sure that an advertising campaign could be directed smack at that Fifth-avenue haberdasher who, surrounded by his stock of tartan scarves, regimental ties and imported English shirtings (myself, I had gone in for American socks), observed on hearing my accent, "You're English, aren't you? – how's the Queen?"

If gin is no longer, as it was in George Saintsbury's day, a "humble and much reviled liquid", it is still, as he went on to say, "the most specially English of all spirits". And to drink it pink, with a dash of Angostura, is the most specially English way of taking it.

And yet both those pioneering cocktail parties of C. R. W. Nevinson's and Mr Alec Waugh's were fuelled not with gin but with rum – it must have been a long time after that before rum was again regarded as socially acceptable enough for that sort of party. For the light, dry, white rums –everything has to be light and dry these days, sometimes at the expense of flavour and character – have only much more recently made any impact here, old-established though I know Bacardi to be; and the full, heavy rums were hardly cocktail-party material. At one time, the light rums came only from Cuba, but Bacardi has set up distilleries in Nassau, in Mexico and in Brazil, and because of the trend of taste the distillers of British Guiana, Trinidad, and even of Jamaica, traditionally the home of the heaviest and most pungent rums, have turned their attention to the lighter sort.

It is this kind of rum that makes what to my mind is the

best of all cocktails – the Daïquiri – which consists of three or four parts of white rum to one part of the juice of fresh limes (not lemon juice, which makes a good drink, but not a Daïquiri; not bottled lime juice; and not tinned "frozen-fresh Daïquiri mix") with soft sugar to taste – about a small teaspoonful seems right – shaken vigorously with finely crushed ice, and strained into ice-cold cocktail glasses. Or, as I have counselled with martinis, keep the rum cold and mix in a jug with an ice-container, and you do not need the crushed ice.

Nowadays, there are plenty of rums to choose from, but it is a mistake to use those that are intended as mixers for long drinks – with tonic-water, for instance, fulfilling the role of gin and of vodka. Many of these are excellent of their kind, but not for Daïquiris, which need not only lightness and dryness, but also a marked flavour of rum, which is lacking – deliberately so – in some of the newest brands. I do not know what rum they use for their Daïquiris at the Fonda del Sol in the Time and Life Building on Fifth Avenue – I think it is a Puerto Rican – but those were the best I tasted in New York: the best I have drunk over here were as good, and were made with the Bacardi Carta de Oro. The other light Bacardi brands, and the Imperial White Diamond, from British Guiana, though good in long drinks, I found not quite full enough in flavour for the perfect Daïquiri.

The Daïquiri had long been a favourite cocktail in a small, closed group in the United States – among those rich Easterners, that is, who habitually spend holidays in the Caribbean. But when I was in New York in 1961, it was to find the Daïquiri as frequent as the martini in a very much wider middle-class circle. Clearly, this was because of President Kennedy's known partiality, by then much publicized, like everything else about his and his family's tastes and habits, for a Daïquiri before dinner, though I have wondered sometimes whether there was not also, in those Castro-catastrophic days, a wistful element of national nostalgia in the fashion: Daïquiri is the place where, in 1898, at the outbreak of the Spanish-American War, the United States Marines landed in Cuba.

And then there are the French proprietary short drinks, the names of which enliven gable-ends for passing motorists, not all of whom find life so richly full of wonder as the Yorkshire-man I once met on a day trip to Boulogne, making his first sortie oversea, who had his belief in the funniness of foreigners confirmed once and for all by ordering beer in a café and getting Byrrh.

Many another adventurous Englishman has made his first acquaintance with France's patent aperitifs in a similarly hit-and-miss sort of way, though, and once the initial shock was over some have even relaxed and enjoyed the experience. Dry red wine given a touch of bitterness by the addition of a little quinine, which is what Byrrh is (I am told there is Peruvian bark as well, and other herbs, with perhaps a sus-picion of brandy) is no bad pick-me-up, and a very good appetizer. Like all the aperitifs that come to mind at the moment, it should be served very cold.

I have been surprised to learn that Dubonnet, which is rather cheaper than Byrrh, and has a rather sweeter finish, is also rather stronger. No doubt it is the sweeter aftertaste that drives such as me to take gin in it: I like about one part of gin to two of Dubonnet, except when the day has gone against me, when half-and-half is none too strong. A twist of lemon peel helps, but I do not put ice in if I can be sure that the ingredients were really cold in the first place. Vodka and Dubonnet might well be a good idea, too, but I have never tried it.

Of these wine-and-quinine aperitifs, Cap Corse also has its

devotees, of whom I am not one: there seems to me to be too much taste of vanilla about it – a flavour I enjoy more after dinner than before. Lillet, on the other hand, which is made not from red wine but from white, and is substantially fortified with brandy, is dry and herby, and I like it.

In style and flavour, Lillet verges on the vermouth country, and there is such an immense variety of vermouths that it is difficult to choose among them: the great Italian firms, such as Gancia, Martini and Cinzano, make it all the more confusing by each producing both a dry and a sweet white vermouth as well as the traditional Italian sweet, or bitter-sweet, red. In Italy itself a call for *bianco* produces a white vermouth that is sweeter than the red, whereas if one wants a dry white vermouth after the French style one must ask for *dry*, in English. All of which tends to baffle those of us who have long been used to the idea that white vermouth is dry and French, red vermouth sweet and Italian. Just to make confusion worse confounded, the French firm of Noilly-Prat, which makes a particularly good French vermouth in Marseilles, now makes an Italian vermouth in Turin, while the famous Turin house of Cinzano sets up in Marseilles to turn out Cinzano French.

Carpano Punt e Mes is one of the more interesting of the Italians: it has more of a bitter tang than the others, and I drink it as the Italians do – with a splash of soda, a lump of ice, and a twist of lemon peel. Campari, which is not a vermouth, but is sold as "bitters", simply, is crisper, less cloying, and a pretty pink in colour: I drink this, too, with soda, ice and lemon – it is becoming as universally known as Scotch – but mixed with twice the amount of sweet Italian vermouth and the same additions it becomes an Americano; with equal quantities of gin and Italian, without additions, save for a twist of orange peel, it is a Negroni: these are both safe drinks to order in any Italian café.

It may be that these Italian mixtures taste better in Venice or on the Via Veneto than they do in London or Liverpool, for in England I find myself turning more towards the French vermouths, with a special liking for the pale dry ones of Chambéry, such as are made, respectively, by the two firms Richard and Dolin. At one time, Chambéry was known to hardly anyone here save customers of the old Escargot Bienvenu restaurant in Greek Street, where it was a speciality of the house, and always offered to patrons as they studied the purple-ink, jellygraphed menu. But, such are the geographical quirks of taste and fashion that it was not taken up here in any serious way (even now, one can hardly describe it as being taken up in a big way) until a director of Gilbeys, travelling in the United States on business, discovered his hosts in San Francisco making their martinis with it – its virtue in a martini being that it gives flavour and fragrance without loss of dryness, and without having to overdo the gin – and arranged for his firm to take over the British agency for the Chambéry made by Dolin.

The same house makes a dry Chambéry flavoured with wild Alpine strawberries, and called – may they be forgiven – Chambéryzette. There is another, identical version of the same thing called Nivolet. This is a pale and pretty pink, rather sweeter than the basic Chambéry, but delicately so, not cloyingly, and an admirable appetizer, served either neat or half-and-half with vodka, and in either case very cold.

Various of these short drinks have given me pleasure, or allayed my miseries, at various times – have prepared me for sometimes delicious, sometimes disappointing, dinners abroad, or reconciled me to facing the dark-brown railway hotels of English provincial towns, or worse still, the chromium-plated, scampi-and-Mateus Rosé, half-plastic-timbered pseudo-pubs of the English countryside. But of all before-dinner or café-table drinks what more evocative than those aniseedy sisters, the Greek ouzo and the French Pernod (which is a brand name: Ricard is the same thing, and there are others)? – clouding slowly in the glass as the colourless liquor impinges on the ice, then more quickly as the water is added, half-and-half; the smell and the taste of the one summoning up visions of the cobbled streets of some Attic or Macedonian or island village, bleached under a blazing sky; the smell and the taste of the other recalling the click-clack-click of high heels on a Paris pavement, the sight and the scent of the girls in their summer frocks, and the sensation of being at least a fortnight younger than one really is.

Though in such circumstances I remind myself that although Pernod is the more benign descendant of the wicked wormwoody absinthe that the French government made illegal in 1914, because it was thought to make men mad or vicious or both, Saintsbury and Creighton used to drink it at Oxford – the real thing, indeed – and became professors, respectively of English Literature and of Ecclesiastical History, and Creighton a bishop twice over.

3 · *Beaded Bubbles*

"I only drink champagne to raise me up from the dead," wrote Hilaire Belloc, "– a thing I constantly need." He would have done better, in what I take to be the relevant circumstances, with Alka-Seltzer, which makes up for our not serving bottles of alkalizing mineral waters with our meals, as the French so sensibly do.

My own view of champagne inclines less to Hilaire Belloc's than to that of John Jorrocks, who observed that, "champagne gives one werry gentlemanly ideas". It certainly had lenitive effects on Mr Khrushchev at Epernay in 1960 – a tour of the champagne cellars having been the only trip he had specially asked for when his official visit to France was being planned, and had clung to even after his illness had caused the tour first to be postponed and then cut short.

He arrived late and rather cross from Rheims, where he had been snubbed by the cathedral clergy (who had locked up the spoons) and irritated by M. Jacquinot, Minister of State, whose speech at luncheon left Mr Khrushchev in doubt, he said, whether the Germans had invaded France as aggressors, or been invited as guests.

But Moët and Chandon mollified him, and by the time he had been driven in a little electric train round some of their seventeen miles of cellars, the most extensive in Champagne, his face, if not exactly wreathed in smiles – there is rather a lot of face for that – was giving off little twinkles of good humour.

Count Robert-Jean de Voguë, head of the firm, elicited some of them by quoting old Russian proverbs (which I suspect him of having made up himself) in the speech in which he offered Mr Khrushchev a glass of Moët and Chandon 1893, bottled in 1894, the year of Mr Khrushchev's birth, and was tactful enough not to point out that the reason for choosing a wine made in the year of his conception was that the year of his birth was not all that good. Tact, indeed, abounded among the French; if not in their guest, who said proudly that they grew a wine in the Caucasus (or perhaps he said the Crimea) that they called "champagne", and wasn't that a tribute to the great product of France? The proud families that had made such a fuss about Spanish "champagne" did not bat an eyelid.

I was able on that occasion to essay a glass myself of the 1893, a remarkable wine, full and soft with age, but still superbly drinkable and full of bubble, as I watched Mr Khrushchev being presented with a case of Moët and Chandon's Dom Pérignon – of which more anon – for consumption off the premises, along with a dozen other dozens from the great houses of Champagne. A salute was fired for the by-now-beaming Mr Khrushchev of the corks from three hundred magnums of the best champagnes, held at the "present" by cellarmen, and the distinguished visitor drove away, through a crowd of *champenois* outside, waving little red flags and shouting "KHRUSH-CHEV! KHRUSH-CHEV!" ("We once nearly had a Communist mayor in Epernay," a member of the firm told me), the while La Fanfare des Tonneliers, in blue smocks, peaked *ouvriers'* caps and white pinafores, tooled away at *"Auprès de ma blonde"*. I like to think that at this stage of the proceedings, in the back of his car, Mr Khrushchev was beating time with a bottle of the best.

Since enjoying that opportunity of drinking champagne made by Moët and Chandon in the year of Mr Khrushchev's conception, I have had many an occasion at the Château de Saran, near Epernay, where that hospitable firm keeps open house, to drink the 1898, the 1911 and the 1914 of the same *marque* – remarkable old wines, but as good to drink as they were because they had been left undisturbed in the Moët and Chandon cellars, still with the sediment on their corks, and disgorged only on the day of drinking – champagne of that age that had been disgorged the usual five years or so after bottling, and then sent out into the world, would probably (not certainly: nothing about wine is certain), have been sad, thin stuff compared with these, or dark in colour and *madérisé* in taste, as a mere 1953 was, from another fine champagne firm, when I opened one bottle of it after another, only the other day.

I noticed, for instance, at a luncheon given in 1964 by Mr George Rainbird at his flat overlooking the park, with M. André Simon, Mr Hugh Johnson of *The Sunday Times*, and Mr Patrick Forbes, of Moët and Chandon's London house, as my fellow-guests, that the 1943 and the 1949 Dom Pérignon

(the premium quality of Moët), although in very good condition and highly drinkable, showed their age much more
than did far older champagnes, because they had been bought
commercially and had been disgorged so much longer ago,
and the 1921, although full and flavoury, with plenty of
bubble, was noticeably *madérisé*. When Mr Patrick Forbes
and his partners, Mr Lawrence Venn and Mr Cyril Maby,
themselves gave a Moët luncheon in a private room at the
Café Royal in July 1964 (the menu, the wine list and the
labels from the bottles have been framed and now hang in the
foyer of the restaurant), the 1914 (from grapes gathered as the
Uhlans jingled through Champagne), and the 1928 both
showed brilliantly in the glass, with never a whiff of *madérisation* in taste or in colour. But they had been disgorged and
liqueured in Epernay only about a fortnight earlier.

The Rheims and Epernay experts – many of whom laugh
at the taste of some Englishmen for old champagne – tell me
that what one enjoys in these historic wines is the softness:
they are not *positively* sweeter than the fresher, crisper 1961s
or non-vintage champagnes that we are drinking now, but
they are relatively or negatively sweeter in that with bottle-
age they have lost acidity. Certainly, most of those I have
mentioned went beautifully with fruit, or with elaborate confections of pastry and cream after dinner, whereas I have
always considered that the current champagnes, blended to
the more usual English taste, are too dry for that, whatever
the books may say about drinking champagne throughout
the meal – counsel that I have never been able to accept. The
champagnes currently available in this country, most of them
brut – except for the few "rich" or *demi-sec* brands, such as
Lanson Rich and Veuve Clicquot Rich – are delicious as
aperitifs, which is the best way of all, to my mind, to drink
champagne, but far too dry to go with fruit or pudding. For

that, if I am to drink sparkling wine, I prefer either the sweet champagnes I have mentioned, which few of my friends would think of serving, or the Italian Asti Spumante, which is not only sweet, but fragrant with the scent of the muscat grape.

There is merit in Asti Spumante, though I know that it is not *chic* to say so. During the campaign in Italy, I used to share a morning bottle with two other correspondents: its fizz gave us the courage to go as far forward for a story as, say, divisional headquarters, and the sugar content gave us the energy to write it when we had got it. And at five shillings or so a bottle, in those days, between the three of us, our respective editors could hardly jib at our expense accounts.

All the same, I used to think it odd that M. Swann should have sent a case of it to Aunt Céline and Aunt Flora, unless it was the rather condescending notion of, "one of the smartest members of the Jockey Club, a particular friend of the Comte de Paris and of the Prince of Wales, and one of the men most sought after in the aristocratic world of the Faubourg Saint-Germain", that a sweet, fizzy wine would be just the thing for a couple of elderly maiden ladies living in the country.

But I came to learn that France always was, and still is, Italy's best foreign customer for Asti Spumante, and we know that long after the time of which Proust was writing – those childhood days at Combray were in the late 1870s or earliest '80s – the French taste in champagne itself, even in the most sophisticated circles, was to drink it sweet. This was confirmed for me not long ago by a chance discovery in an Edinburgh bookshop. Side-by-side, on a shelf devoted to books about eating and drinking, I found the first edition and the third of *The Gourmet's Guide to Europe*; the one published in 1903 and described as being, "by Lieut.-Col. Newnham-Davis and Algernon Bastard, edited by the former"; the other published in 1911, with no reference on the title-page to Mr Bastard (who is thought by Mr Raymond Postgate – an authority on Newnham-Davis, the "Dwarf of Blood", as on so much else – to have been nothing more than a soldierly jest of the gallant colonel's), but a note in the preface recording with much regret his death.

I had always wanted a copy of what, in its modest way, is a pioneer work, and I suppose a serious bibliophile would have been satisfied with the first edition. Finding, though, that the one copy cost only three shillings, and the other no more than four, I decided to hang the expense and take the two. My excuse to myself for my extravagance was that there might be illuminating differences between the gastronomic Europe of 1903 and that of 1911.

Even without any very scholarly collation of the two editions, I was soon justified. I found the colonel observing in 1903 that, "as to the champagnes found abroad, unless they are specially made for the English market, they must not be judged from an English standpoint, being as a rule far too sweet for our taste." And he went on to recall staying at Rheims, "for some shooting owned by a syndicate of some of the larger champagne shippers. We met for *déjeuner* at their Châlet de Chasse or club-house, each gentleman bringing his own wine. The result was that one saw from ten to a dozen different famous brands of champagne on the table.

"My host asked me which sort I would prefer. '*Du vin Brut*, if you have any,' I replied. '*Ah! Vous buvez de ce poison-là?*' exclaimed he, smiling. So they evidently did not agree with our taste for dry wine."

Nowadays, of course, the taste of French champagne-shippers – of any serious French drinker of champagne, indeed – is at least as austere as that of those good customers, the English, and I wondered when the change took place. To my delight, I found that the whole anecdote had been omitted from the 1911 edition and not, presumably, simply on grounds of space, for the third edition is twice as long as the first, and it was so good a story that I think the author would only have cut it out because it had become dated.

I had not realized before that the French were still drinking their champagne sweet so relatively recently, but sure enough, when I consulted M. André Simon's *History of Champagne*, I found that although the cult of heavily sugared champagne came to an end in England in the '70s, champagne was still a sweet dessert wine in France in the '90s. The story in the first edition of the *Gourmet's Guide* supports this view precisely: the champagne party recalled in 1903 probably took place a couple of years before. What is surprising is the apparent suddenness of the change, but the story justifies Swann's gift of Asti: we know that he visited Italy frequently, bringing back "photographs of the old masters" for Marcel, so that he would be familiar with the wine, even if he did not meet it often in the Faubourg, and he would hardly find it too sweet, for it would be sweet champagne that he was drinking at *le Jockey* and the tables of the great.

The dryness or sweetness of champagne, unlike that of still table wines, is completely controllable. When the sediment that has been encouraged to settle on the cork is disgorged, the tiny space left in the bottle is filled by "liqueuring" – by adding something between an ounce and a half and two ounces of old champagne in which a little cane sugar has been dissolved. On the amount of sugar depends whether the champagne will be *brut, sec,* or *demi-sec*. These words denote relative degrees of dryness, *brut* being the driest – it really means "natural", or unsweetened, though I doubt whether there is any champagne at all without *some* sweetening, or whether it would be palatable if there were.

Very slight differences in the amount of sugar in the liqueuring will make considerable differences in the "style" of the champagne. Expressed in percentages, one would mean a very dry wine indeed, four a sweet, and seven a very sweet one. What pre-revolutionary nobs in St Petersburg used to drink from the slippers of the Maryinsky ballerinas was twelve or more per cent – a champagne so rich that it had to be specially confected for the Russian market. They tell me in Rheims and Epernay that nobody in Western Europe would drink a champagne as sweet as that, though the sparkling wines of the Crimea follow the old tradition in catering for the cold-climate conviviality of Moscow and Leningrad. Sharply cold climates always do call for sweeter wines – Scandinavia imports champagnes that are much sweeter than we drink, in our soft and muggy island. Compare with that 12 per cent, though, Pol Roger Rich and Lanson Rich (which the French would call *demi-sec*): they are delicious with dessert, but far too sweet for most English tastes as an aperitif, or with meat or fish. Yet they are only three and a half and four per cent respectively.

The figures I give vary a little, of course, from time to time, and from vintage to vintage. In a "big" year, the liqueuring will not need to be quite so sweet as in a year when the grapes have more acid and less sugar. Also, a young wine needs more liqueuring than even a very slightly older one: "when one starts shipping a vintage," one shipper has told me, "there would be a fractionally bigger *dosage* than a few years later, when one might still be shipping the same vintage". The disgorgement takes place only just before shipment, and the liqueuring, or *dosage*, is varied to maintain the house-style.

It must be borne in mind, too, in any consideration of the age and the sweetness of champagne, that national taste changes, as it has done in this country within the past half-century. Lanson tells me, for example, that at the turn of the century champagne was shipped and drunk quite young: I have seen an invoice for champagne they supplied to Edward VII at Sandringham, shipped four years after the vintage and not, it would seem, for laying down. (The 1898 Moët was served at the Coronation banquet of 1902.) Then there came a period during which the English drank champagne when it was what the French regarded as past its best – eight years old, and even ten to fifteen. Now the wheel has turned full circle, and five years is quite normal for a vintage champagne.

Not only younger, but even a shade sweeter. It was in the 1850s and 1860s, according to M. André Simon, that the English began to develop their taste for a wine much drier than that enjoyed in Champagne itself, but George Saintsbury, in his *Notes on a Cellar-Book* (1920), wrote that the change from sweet to dry "was not finally accomplished when my Cellar-Book was started", which was in 1884. By the end of the century, though, the *goût anglais* was well-established: we drank our champagne drier than anyone else in the world.

Now, according to the shippers of Heidsieck Dry Monopole, there has been the merest whisper of a swing the other way: we still drink our champagne dry, but a very little less dry than we used to do. Dry Monopole used to have from half to three-quarters of one per cent liqueuring – now it is one per cent.

When the late Winston Churchill joined his regiment, seventy years ago, the commanding officer was a Colonel Brabazon who, between having been a regimental officer in the Brigade of Guards and taking up command of the 4th

Hussars, had served in a line regiment, the name of which he said, "I never can wemember, but they wear gween facings, and you get at 'em fwom Waterloo". And it was in much the same spirit and tone of voice that he once asked an irascible mess president, "And which chemist do you get this champagne fwom?" One does not have to be invited to many weddings to learn to sympathize with the late Colonel Brabazon, and yet there is no excuse for anyone's serving bad champagne in this country, where there is more good champagne available than anywhere in the world save France itself, and where every wine-merchant, however modest, has one or two of the great names on his list, and perhaps a cheaper one as well, with a label of his own on it. There are know-alls who disparage them, but some of these "b. o. b." champagnes are very good. They are so called because they come from houses in Champagne that specialize in wines to be sold as "buyer's own brand", and some of these firms are very highly respected in the trade, and have dealt with similarly distinguished firms here for generations. One that I have long admired is that of de Venoge, in Epernay: the Savoy lists its wine (under that name) in its excellent list, and the Lambert sold by Morgan Furze of Brick Street comes from the same source, and is similarly light and elegant in style. I have never had a bad bottle of either. The Lambert *blanc de blancs* – made from white grapes only, instead of the usual three or so parts of black to one of white, and therefore particularly delicate – is on the list of the Directors' Wine Club, of which I am on the board, and so I drink a good deal of it, and come to little harm.

But it is the fifteen or sixteen *"grandes marques"** that are

* In Britain, this phrase is generally used to denote the wines of one or other of the most distinguished and best-known houses – I think that Ayala, Bollinger, Veuve Clicquot, Heidsieck Dry Monopole, Charles Heidsieck, Irroy, Krug,

household names, and choosing between them is a matter of personal taste, for they do not vary so much in quality – all the great houses make good champagne – as in style. Thus, that excellent, old-fashioned wine, Bollinger, is full-flavoured and fruity, for all its dryness – a champagne with the body to stand up to food (for those who, unlike me, cling to the belief that champagne is a wine that can be drunk throughout a meal) as is the similarly dry but rather full Heidsieck Dry Monopole. At the other end of the scale are the lighter, "crisper", brands, such as Moët and Chandon, Mumm Cordon Rouge and Irroy, more suitable if the wine is to be drunk as an aperitif – and there is no better aperitif in the world.

So everyone has his favourite champagne – Winston Churchill, for instance, was devoted throughout his long lifetime to Pol Roger, which falls between Bollinger and the Mumms in style; Mr Nubar Gulbenkian, who is rather richer than I am, used to swear by Krug, the most expensive of champagnes, until he began to find that noble wine rather

Lanson, Mercier, Moët and Chandon, Mumm, Perrier-Jouët, Piper-Heidsieck, Pol Roger, Pommery, Roëderer and Taittinger are the lot. But in France there is a Syndicat de Grandes Marques (*de*, rather than *des*, signifying that it is not exhaustive), which Mr Maurice Buckmaster, public relations officer of the champagne trade, characteristically described to me as being, "a kind of club that might reasonably be compared with 'Pop' at Eton." It is pretty particular about whom it elects – Mercier, the latest to be elected, at the end of 1964, took a long time to get in, and met some pretty resolute resistance – and is not to be confused with the Syndicat des Commerçants de Champagne, which is purely a selling organization. Some English shippers hold that the term, "*grandes marques*," should apply only to the twelve or thirteen houses that run the Champagne Academy course for young entrants to the trade: the list I have given, but not including Ayala, Irroy, Piper-Heidsieck, Taittinger or – I think – Mercier. To paraphrase Mr Buckmaster's analogy, it is rather like the term, "public school," in this country, which may sometimes mean all schools represented in the Headmasters' Conference, and sometimes a much smaller and more self-conscious group, all according to context.

heavy and full-bodied for him, and took to the lighter, drier Richard de Ayala (not to be confused with that other eminent champagne labelled Ayala, simply), made by his brother-in-law of that name. Failing that – for it is not easy to come by – he favours Pommery, and M. André Simon, with a beaming smile, shoudlers a Churchillian burden of years on the same admirable wine. All good judges.

Myself – to descend to a less exalted level – I have good reason for liking Moët, which is made well and shipped with care by good friends of mine; as is Pol Roger, which is the champagne served exclusively at a small dining-club I know, where I have eaten good food, downed many a delicious bottle, and listened to good talk, for Mr Denzil Batchelor is of the company; and as is Lanson Black Label, which I always choose when entertaining those who might find champagne "too acid", for although it is far from sweet, it is a whisper less dry than most – it has about one and three quarter per cent liqueuring as against the one to one and a half per cent more usual in *brut* champagnes, and the four of Lanson Rich.

Generally speaking, the vintage champagne of each *marque* is rather fuller and fruitier than the non-vintage of the same name, and costs a few shillings more a bottle – with the Krug non-vintage about the same price as most of the other houses' vintage.

The fuller-bodied champagnes appeal to older-fashioned tastes, and they are usually those that are made in an older-fashioned way. For there is a great debate in progess in Champagne between those who believe that the steadily increasing world demand must be met by modern methods – hydraulic presses, more and speedier conveyor-belts in bottling-plants, stainless-steel tanks for first fermentation (second fermentation *must*, of course, be in bottle) – and those who cling to wooden casks, and the ancient, unhurried ways.

Count Robert-Jean de Vogüe of Moët and Chandon (which, with an output of more than six million bottles a year, is the biggest producer of all, and outsells all its rivals, both at home and abroad), is the spokesman for the innovators. "Either we expand, like every other twentieth-century industry," he says, "or the world will have to get along without champagne." Meaning, of course, that the sparkling-wine producers of Germany, Italy and Spain, with no inhibitions at all about modernizing, and lacking both the tradition of the champagne-makers and the stricter sanctions of France's laws of *appellation*, which in this case prevent any sacrifice of quality for the sake of quantity, will swamp the market through sheer efficiency and the lower prices that this makes possible. And he goes on to point out that modern methods mean more precise control of what are still natural processes.

Madame Bollinger, on the other hand, whose family firm produces fewer than a million bottles a year, will not have anything but oak for first fermentation, ages her non-vintage wine for five years instead of the obligatory three, and throws up her hands in horror at what she calls the "brutality" of the innovators.

Temperamentally, I am on the side of the conservatives (in matters of food and wine, if not of politics) but there is much in what they say at Moët and Chandon, the wine of which is just as good, of its lighter, crisper kind, as is the fuller-bodied, older-style wine of Madame Bollinger outstanding in its kind – I prefer it not only to that of Mercier, a similarly progressive house, but also to that of many of the smaller and more traditional producers. Partly, this is because its fresh, dry style happens to be to my taste (I consider the firm's Dom Pérignon to be one of the two or three greatest champagnes of all), but I can also praise its consistency of character and quality, which may well be the result of the closer control made possible by modern processes. Champagne is, after all, a blended wine (black grapes and white; the grapes of different vineyards; and, in non-vintage champagne, the wine of different years);* is deliberately induced to undergo a second fermentation; and then sweetened, in the liqueuring process that replaces the wine lost when its deposits are expelled. As it is to this extent not an entirely natural product, anyway, who is to say at what precise point the control of natural processes must stop, so long as the wine is honestly made, and pleasing?† French law takes good care that the grapes must be such, pruned in such a way, grown in this place and not that, producing not more than so much wine to the acre, their juice fermented naturally, and for the second time in bottle, not in tanks, or in any other way than the manner laid down. What the new men are doing is not altering any of that, but simply seeing that what *is* allowed shall be done as efficiently as possible. The same sort of thing is being done in Bordeaux and in Burgundy, to make red wines mature more quickly than they used to do, and I see nothing wrong in that, and much that is to everyone's benefit.

Nobody takes pink champagne very seriously: most of the classic books on French wines ignore it, and even in M. André Simon's great recent work, *The History of Champagne*, there is only the briefest reference. A pity, for a lot of care and expense go into its making, and it is produced by people who know how to handle fine wines.

Nothing could look more festive for a party. Yet it has its

---

* Even a vintage champagne may include a small, legally limited, amount of the wine of another vintage, if the style and character of a wine demand it. The heavy 1959s all had as much as the law allowed of the wines of lighter years.

† I do not suggest that there is anything *artificial* about champagne: only natural wine and natural processes are involved, but they are induced, controlled and manipulated.

serious side. I have drunk a dry 1953 Veuve Clicquot rosé as an accompaniment to a rich dish of fish done with butter and mushrooms, and found it admirable – dry enough for the dish, and the colour setting it off as a white wine would not.

I learned from the eminent firm that makes it that this was the first rosé it had offered since 1937, because it was the first year since then that the grapes had been exactly right for the job. A fair enough measure of how seriously a serious firm can take this supposedly frivolous wine – what may be another indication being that it costs many shillings a bottle more than the white of the same vintage.

There are two respectable ways of producing a pink champagne: either in the same way as any other *vin rosé*, by leaving the juice on the skins of the grapes it has been pressed from just long enough to become pink, but not to become red (virtually all champagne is made from about 80 per cent black grapes to about 20 per cent white – the exact proportion varying slightly according to the vintage); or by adding a carefully calculated amount of the still red wine of the region (Bouzy) to a vintage white champagne before the fermentation in bottle. This is the only method mentioned in M. Simon's book. The reason why Veuve Clicquot, who stick to the first method, did not make a rosé between 1937 and 1953 is that not until then were the black grapes at exactly the ripeness, when the vintage came, to give the colour without too much tannin.

Most of the *grande marque* houses that make pink champagne at all take it so seriously – more so, certainly, than the people who drink it – that they make only vintage rosé, and no non-vintage.

In recent years, I have tasted the 1955 Irroy, Moët and Chandon, and Taittinger, and found them all fresh, fragrant, and with a good deep colour – the Taittinger perhaps the blandest, the Moët the lightest, and the Irroy the fruitiest, though the differences between the three wines were very slight, and possibly only to be detected when all three were tasted together.

Two of the *grande marque* houses – Heidsieck Dry Monopole and Lanson – each make a non-vintage pink champagne, which is consequently that much cheaper than the others: the Dry Monopole is the deeper in colour, the Lanson very light, both rather less dry than some, as is the Mercier, though all are fresh and clean on the palate, for no pink champagne is at all sweet, though I fancy that the pink Lanson is rather more so than its white cousin, the Lanson Black Label.

But if pink champagne is rather out of fashion, *blanc de blancs* is rather in, in spite of those – some of them, perhaps, members of firms that do not make one – who claim that all you need to do, to make a *blanc de blancs*, is to give the appropriate order to the man who prints your labels. But there is a real thing, and it is made by using the juice of white grapes only, instead of the more usual four parts or so of black to one of white. In the conventional champagne, the black grapes give body and flavour, the white grapes finesse and delicacy, so that a good *blanc de blancs* is especially light and delicate, in tune with the modern taste in drinks, and eminently suitable as an aperitif or at parties.

I have already mentioned the Lambert *blanc de blancs*, and Mercier make one that is similarly light and fresh – suitable, I once suggested in an article in *The Observer*, for drinking out of the slippers of the smaller sort of chorus girl, where the more plentiful, more flavoury and more conventional *blanc et noir* was better adapted for launching all ships larger than a corvette, and for the walking-shoes of Dames of the British Empire.

The Taittinger *blanc de blancs* (now labelled with the brand name, Comtes de Champagne) has been given the social climber's accolade of a mention in the James Bond novels, which if it were not as good as it is – the 1959 is delightfully fresh and elegant for so heavy a year – would be enough to bar it from my table. But then Ian Fleming (who was once my immediate superior, when he was Foreign Manager for Kemsley Newspapers, and I was the Moscow correspondent of *The Sunday Times*) knew nothing about wine, except what he was told when he rang up friends in the wine trade, and then usually got it wrong. The Regency Club in New York (based on the Knickerbocker, perhaps?) is supposed to have made James Bond's Blades Club in St James's (based on Boodle's?) a present of Dom Pérignon 1946, which is impossible, because 1946 was not a vintage in Champagne – and in one of the novels Piesporter Goldtröpfchen, from the Mosel, is referred to as a hock.

The very special prestige brands made by a couple of the most notable houses are not quite *blanc de blancs*, but very nearly – I think that Dom Pérignon is made, according to the year, with approximately 80 per cent white grapes to 20 black, the reverse of the usual proportions. This is a particularly graceful wine, appropriately put up in a pretty replica of the traditional eighteenth-century champagne bottle: it has been much sought after by American millionaires since before its mention in the Bond canon, and I love it dearly, which is the proper adverb, I fancy, for a bottle that at the time of writing costs well over fifty shillings. Roëderer Cristal Brut is a shade fuller than the Dom Pérignon, equally distinguished, and about the same price.

Recently, one of the most highly regarded of all the great champagne houses has joined their ranks – but with a difference. Where other "premium" champagnes owe their character to differences in blend from the normal *cuvées* of the same brands – a higher proportion of white grapes to black, say, or a particularly careful selection of the very best grapes – Bollinger's new "Réserve" is a late-disgorged vintage wine. Madame Bollinger, with whom I first drank it at her home in Ay, says proudly that she could not select better grapes than she always uses, or make a better-balanced blend. The difference in this new special champagne is that whereas the normal vintage and non-vintage Bollinger is disgorged – rid of its sediment – some four or five years after bottling, the Réserve waits ten or twelve.

A longer spell on its sediment means greater softness and mellowness in champagne, whereas age in bottle after disgorgement can often mean a loss of freshness and bubble, and a greater depth of colour – perhaps *madérisation*.

I tasted the newly-disgorged 1955 Réserve at Ay in 1966 – a wine that would normally have been disgorged in 1959 or 1960 – and, at that splendid Paris restaurant, Lasserre, the 1953 Réserve, proudly labelled as having been disgorged on January 25, 1965. Both were bland and mellow, to nose and to palate, with a rather more subdued bubble than the ordinary vintage wine would have shown, but still lively and with the true Bollinger character, and far greater freshness than one would meet in champagnes of the same age that had been disgorged – as they would normally have been – some half-dozen years earlier.

All these prestige wines are superb, but not, I suppose, for everyday drinking – not at my income level, anyway. Whereas a merciful Providence has ordained that some champagnes, at any rate, shall be shipped in quarter-bottles, and something a little less than ten shillings for a quarter-bottle of Pommery, say, is a modest sum for a sizeable mid-morning quencher. And I wish more restaurants did as they do at the Café Royal, where quarter-bottles of Ayala and of Perrier-Jouët are available for the solitary diner to console himself with as he studies the menu. But quarter-bottles are not for laying down: they have been decanted from full-size bottles, and do not keep well. Nor, indeed, are they necessary at home: there are two or three kinds of bottle-stopper that will keep the fizz and the freshness in an opened bottle of champagne for days on end.

Lately, the Connaught Rooms, where they sell thousands of bottles of champagne a year, have been suggesting in their advertisements that "a new way to drink it" is to have it in a silver tankard. With all respect both to the Connaught Rooms and to their excellent Champagne Bar this is not so new a way as all that. More than one London club has been serving champagne in silver or in pewter tankards since Edwardian times and even earlier – my own club has poured much Bollinger into silver for me in this way, to the delight, when he dined with me there, of Mr Ronald Barton, of Langoa and Léoville, who likes, when in England, to live in an English – indeed, in an old-fashioned English – way.

For some reason that I do not understand, metal seems to give the wine an entirely different taste from what it has in glass – neither a better taste nor a worse, but different. I enjoy it in a tankard as a mid-morning drink, or as a pick-me-up in a wine bar, but I prefer it in a glass at a party, or before a meal.

Not, for choice, in one of those shallow, saucer-like glasses that the French call *coupes*: they are ugly in themselves, fit only for ice-cream, and let the bubbles dissipate too quickly. The tall, very narrow *flute* is elegant, but holds too little wine: the best glass I know of for champagne is similarly tall, but tulip-shaped, so that there is a fair amount of "belly" in the middle to hold a decent few mouthfuls of wine, but with a narrower top, so that not too much of the champagne is exposed to the air, which is what causes it to lose its bubbles quickly, and so that the "nose" of the wine is not lost.

I was once made to look very foolish over the wretched *coupes*. It was in the course of a press visit to Cognac, and I had been showing off to the then *Financial Times* man – among many other things, about my knowledge of French drinking habits. That flat, saucer-shaped champagne glass for example, I said, was not only unsuitable, but it was peculiarly English – you would never see a Frenchman using it.

That very evening, we dined, uncommonly well, at the splendid château of one of the Hennessy family, and there on the table, of course, were the flat, saucer-shaped *coupes* that I had sworn you would never find in France! Our host agreed that they were, indeed, rare among his fellow-countrymen, and I think he must have got them in England – perhaps for that very reason.

Not long after we got back I turned up an article by Mr James Laver, who knows so much about the history of taste and fashion, in wines and table appointments as well as in clothes. Among the illustrations was a menu cover designed by "Sem" for one of the smart Bois de Boulogne restaurants of the very early 1900s: Mr Laver observes of it that, "the English custom of taking champagne in shallow saucer-like glasses has never found favour in France, as can be seen from this illustration", which shows champagne being drunk from what I suppose we would call claret glasses.

The only notable wine-amateur of our time who still defends the *coupe* is the octogenarian Mr H. Warner Allen, who has written that he likes, "the generous expanse of golden wine it presents", whereas the equally distinguished and even more venerable M. André Simon considers it, "anything but ideal . . . not giving the wine a fair chance to keep and show off its bubbles".

M. Simon goes a long way towards establishing, in his great book on the history of champagne, that the *coupe* was in fact designed and first made in England, specifically for champagne, as long ago as 1663. His own preference is not for the tapering *flute*, either, which is much used in France, but for the half-opened-tulip shape, on a longish stem, that I have already mentioned as my own first choice, and to be found very cheaply at most glass shops.

M. Simon, who not only knows more about wine than probably any other living man, but more about champagne than about any other wine (he was the Pommery representative over here more than sixty years ago, and for half a lifetime, and his first book was about champagne), writes that he once used pint mugs made of crystal glass, with stars engraved in the base from which the bubbles rose vertically. I do not know why cuts in the internal surface of a glass set the bubbles going, but they do.

Presumably, M. Simon's mugs were meant each to take the contents of one of those old-fashioned imperial-pint bottles, such as inspired one of the most moving tributes to wine ever written in English prose – the passage in Duff Cooper's *Old Men Forget* about wine as, "a firm friend and a wise counsellor", – in which the author recalled having been heartened on a wet Sunday evening in 1917, in what I take to have been the Royal Automobile Club, by "an imperial pint of champagne, that admirable measure which like so many good things has disappeared from the world".

The particular wine that Private Cooper drank that evening over his copy of *Alice Through the Looking Glass* (I think that they were privates in those days, and not guardsmen) was Veuve Clicquot, and it is true that this splendid wine has not been available here in imperial pints since just after the last war. But Krug, Roëderer, Bollinger, Perrier-Jouët, Pol

Roger and Lanson are among those great houses that still ship "that admirable measure" – between the half-bottle (which is sometimes called a pint, but is not an imperial pint) and the bottle, but nearer to the bottle size, and not to be confused with the huge *impériale* of Bordeaux.

All the same, the measure is nothing like so popular as it was: that is why the shippers of Veuve Clicquot gave it up, and a director of the firm that ships Lanson Black Label also tells me that the demand for imperial pints is very limited. A pity – here is the perfect measure for two people sharing a light luncheon or, as Private Cooper discovered, for the solitary diner on a gloomy evening.*

The imperial pint was a great Edwardian favourite, and Harry Preston, that Brighton *bon vivant* of the time, used to have one to himself every morning, with a chicken sandwich.

* After these lines were written, I had a letter from Prince de Caraman Chimay in which he told me that when he read Duff Cooper's book (published in 1953), "it happened that I, as head of the Veuve Clicquot firm, had just had the idea of reviving this time-honoured size with the vintage 1947, which was just coming out, and I immediately sent a case to Duff, writing him that at least it was my privilege to make good one of the disasters.

"I got a very charming answer, which, alas, reached me the very day when I read in the papers the sudden death of the writer. And it did not bring good luck to the imperial pints because, as you say, it never became popular – tastes and customs have changed, and the house of Veuve Clicquot has given up showing them. The days when the imperial pint was the ideal drink for a happy couple, home after theatre, or the lonely bachelor in his club, are gone."

That "very charming" letter of thanks for the case of imperial pints of Veuve Clicquot must have been one of the very last things – perhaps even the very last – that Duff Cooper wrote, and it may be that Prince de Caraman Chimay should persuade his successors to reconsider their decision, and produce a few cases of imperial pints every year, with a black border to the label, in memory of Duff Cooper, as Pol Roger has done ever since the death of Winston Churchill, its most famous patron.

Is there, by the way, any parallel to Pol Roger's gesture, in the wine trade or in any other? I know that the R.R. on Rolls-Royce motor cars turned from red to black, but that was in mourning for a head of the firm, not for a customer.

But champagne was cheaper in those days. Chicken tasted of something, too, come to that.

So far as I know, Bollinger is the only house to mature its champagne in double magnums as well as in magnums (which are double bottles), bottles, imperial pints, and halves. Some people call these double magnums jeroboams; others reserve the name for bottles not four but six times the normal size. It all depends on whether a rehoboam holds six bottles or eight, or whether the eight-bottle size is a methusaleh.

There is nothing serious or time-hallowed, though, about anything bigger than a double magnum – certainly not about the salmanazar (twelve bottles), balthazar (sixteen), and nebuchadnezzar (twenty), all of which are publicity devices for window-dressing or trade fairs, and all of which have to be filled by decanting from magnums, as quarter-bottles are filled from bottles. No champagne that has had to be decanted and recorked is as good as champagne in the bottle in which it has matured, and in which it underwent its secondary fermentation.

But the bigger the bottle in which the wine has been matured, the better and the longer-lived the wine – which means that in Bollinger the double magnum, and in all other marks the magnum, is the best of its kind. When Moët and Chandon decided in 1955 to ferment and mature a little of their Dom Pérignon in magnums, as well as in bottles and halves, it was only for their "library" of fine wines, intended for special family occasions, after long ageing – encouraged to do so by the remarkable quality shown at that time by the 1928 and 1929 vintage Moët in magnums, compared with the same wine in bottles. But this 1955 trial run was such a success that it was repeated on a more commercial scale in 1959 and 1961, and now about five per cent of the total production of Dom Pérignon goes into the double bottles. In 1966, I drank the 1959 from both the magnum and the bottle, and when I observed that I found it hard to detect any difference in quality, I was told that between magnums and bottles of the same champagne the difference in quality begins to show only after about ten years, becoming very marked after about twenty. It is especially noticeable by now, I was told, in the 1952 – a great wine, but much more markedly so in magnums.

Champagne is necessarily expensive – not because its makers and shippers are grasping, but because the process of manufacture is lengthy and requires much labour and particular skills, as well as specially strong bottles and corks, wire and foil, and elaborate cellar appliances. In this country, moreover, the tax on sparkling wine is substantially higher than on still table wine.

All the more reason, therefore, for not swizzling out the bubbles that have been put in (or, rather, induced to put themselves in, by secondary fermentation, and then retained) with so much trouble and at such expense – not even with a gold swizzle-stick, or "mosser", from Aspreys on the end of a gold-and-platinum chain. Perhaps, too, we should disdain to dilute this noble wine into champagne cups and champagne cocktails, though I must confess to a liking, on a hot summer's day, for that innocent refreshment, a mixture of fresh, unsweetened orange-juice (not that sweetened, slimy, tinned stuff), mixed half-and-half, ice-cold, with an equal amount of champagne.

One London club likes to regard this as a speciality of the house, and calls it Buck's Fizz although, under its native name of *champagne-orange*, and in its native place, it is regularly quaffed by many a Frenchman whom Buck's would blackball on sight. Mr Geoffrey Hallowes who, like his father and his grandfather before him, is the personal holder of the British agency for Heidsieck Dry Monopole, confesses that whatever the purists may say, he not only delights in Buck's Fizz on a hot summer's day, but that when he was in Singapore he found that champagne served very cold with a sprig of fresh mint in the glass was similarly refreshing. And the aperitif of the house at the excellent Michelin-starred Grand Hotel Clément, at Ardres, just the other side of Calais (near enough for those of us who live near Lydd airport to have visited occasionally for luncheon in the days, now no more, alas, when there was a Lydd-Calais service) is a finger of the particularly good *crème de framboise* (not the colourless *eau-de-vie*, but the sweet, fruity raspberry cordial) that the estimable M. Gantelme buys especially from a small producer in Burgundy, in a tall glass, filled with ice-cold champagne – a luxurious, sparkling variant of *vin blanc cassis*.

These are light-hearted mixtures. I take much more seriously Black Velvet, which consists of half champagne, half Guinness, served very cold, and preferably in silver tankards. Real champagne, mind you, and real Guinness – sweet stout and Babycham make Black Velveteen, and may the Lord forgive you.

I refer not Lord Boyd, Lord Moyne, Lord Iveagh or Lord Elveden, but to an even better-known Lord.

George Saintsbury, although he wrote of, "that noble liquor called of Guinness" as, "the comeliest of black malts", said of Black Velvet (which was called Bismarck in his time – I cannot think why: where would Bismarck have got hold of Guinness?) that the stout overwhelms the champagne, "and all the wine does is to make the beer more intoxicating and more costly. Thus the thing is at once vicious and vulgar". This is snobbish nonsense: it is equally true, and more important, that on a cold day the stout gives body to the wine and, appropriately for a party, the wine gives sparkle to the beer. Anyway, it was Gerald du Maurier's favourite tipple, and he was a much nicer man than George Saintsbury. I like it, too, and so am I.

No wine has ever earned so many or such affectionate nicknames from the English, who have always been among the greatest consumers of champagne.* The derivation of "fizz" and "bubbly" is self-evident, and "the widow" commemorates the Veuve Clicquot. It came to be called "the boy" by Edwardian and late-Victorian heavy swells after a shooting-party – the story goes – at which Edward VII (when Prince of Wales) was present, at which a lad trundled a wheelbarrow-load of champagne around, packed in ice. It was a hot day, and the number of times the thirsty guns called "Boy!" led to a transference of epithet from the lad himself to what he had charge of.

Not that it always followed, as a late-Victorian social historian primly observed, "that everybody who uses the word nowadays was out shooting that day with the Prince". But who calls it "the boy" today? All I ever hear nowadays is "champers". Which is unimaginative of us, I suppose, but then I doubt whether even the most relentlessly facetious present-day after-dinner speaker would stoop to the early-Victorian toast I came across in *The Toastmaster's Companion: Loyal, Patriotic, Naval, Military, Love, Bottle, Masonic, Sporting and other Toasts and Sentiments:*

Champaign to our real friends, and
Real pain to our sham friends.

* Great Britain imports well over five million bottles a year, as against the United States' three and a half million, which makes ours the most valuable export market, though measured by consumption per head, with nine bottles to every hundred of us, we are out-guzzled by Belgium, with eighteen, and Switzerland, helped by her visiting tourists, with thirteen, to say nothing of France herself, with one for every man, woman, and child.

4 · Sweet and Dry

A few years ago, my wife and I were entertained to luncheon at one of the great first-growth châteaux of Barsac, famous even among its famous neighbours for the splendour of its sweet, golden wine. The other guests included some of the most noted sweet-wine growers of Barsac and Sauternes.

With each delicious course we were served a bigger, fruitier, sweeter wine than the last, until with the roast gigot of mutton we were drinking that honey-sweet and scented miracle, Château d'Yquem 1921.

"Don't you think our white wines here are very pretty?" my host inquired – no doubt because I had forborne to comment, and he had hoped for compliments.

"Oh yes," I assured him: "Oh yes, indeed I do" – wondering how I was ever going to complete so liverish a meal, and thinking how much more I could have enjoyed that fabulous wine with a meltingly ripe peach or with the juiciest of pears, and how nobly the mutton would have been accompanied by a bottle of claret from only a few miles downstream.

"I knew you'd agree with me," said my host: "What d'you think of those fellows in the Médoc, drinking those sour red wines of theirs?"

What wines go with what dishes is largely governed in France, as it is not governed here at all, by geography and by parochial patriotism, and such a meal as I recall is frequent in the Sauternais. Professor J.-R. Roger, of the Académie du Vin de France, in his book *The Wines of Bordeaux*, published here in translation in 1960, selected from several examples of Sauternes dinners the 1926 banquet at Château d'Yquem as, "a meal which was considered quite perfect and is still quoted as a model of its kind:

Consommé en tasse
Langouste à la Sévigné
Aiguillettes de Canetons à l'orange
Filet froid à la façon de Périgord
Asperges nouvelles
Salade de saison
Parfait Trianon
Dessert

LES VINS
Château Filhot 1904
Château d'Yquem 1914
Château d'Yquem 1921
Château d'Yquem 1869

"Notice that the three Château d'Yquems are great vintages: the 1914 not so rich and luscious as the celebrated 1921 and 1869, but very fine and elegant all the same."

The 1921 Yquem was a young wine then, and became a legend. I have drunk it twice since my Sauternais luncheon, on both occasions in London, with fruit, and therefore with greater enjoyment: the last time as recently as the autumn of 1966, when it was still full of sweetness and at an age when other great Sauternes are tired and *madérisé*. But what I remember best about it is the story I was told by a woman acquaintance, early in the war, who had just been divorced, and to her great surprise, by her much older and, hitherto, complaisant husband.

They had lived, she and the husband, in a stately Sussex home, the park of which had been turned by the War Office into a tented field, and its greater rooms into the officers' mess of a smart and rather rakish regiment.

Its subalterns were not indifferent to the lady's charms; the lady herself not unduly prim, nor hard to please. It was somehow understood that neither the colonel nor the cuckolded husband would complain, so long as certain decencies – or, to be more precise, certain reticences – were observed.

And yet . . . the blow fell. The lady and that evening's lover were discovered, when on other evenings with other young men, her adventures had gone carefully unnoticed. She was turned out into the black-out at little more than a moment's notice, and divorced as quickly as a lady can be.

It was long before she could understand why, she told me. Why that evening, and not on any other? And then it had dawned on her. Until that particular evening, she had dispensed her favours, by previous and prettily planned arrangement, in boudoir or in bedroom. It was an understood thing, and the eyes both of martial and of marital authority had winked at it. But on the particular, the fatal, evening she was showing off the house to a recently joined young officer, and they had reached the wine cellar which, in that house, was very properly a show-place. A look in his hostess's eye overwhelmed the boy; his ardour would not wait; and they were heard, and thus discovered, in such a position, she shyly intimated, as to be agitating the bin of Yquem 1921.

So localized are the wine-drinking habits of the French that even "those fellows in the Médoc" drink the full sweet wines of the region with the local *pâté de foie gras des Landes* (which is always served as a middle course, between fish and entrée) on the principle that full, rich food needs to be matched by a full, rich wine, but this is a combination that I find cloying in the extreme. On the other hand, I was interested to find, at a luncheon given not long ago by Mr David Burns and Mr William Warre, two young Masters of Wine who are directors of George Idle, Chapman, (who ship Dow's port, among much else of merit) the smoked salmon accompanied by a 1926 Rayne-Vigneau, a first growth of Sauternes, still showing a beautiful golden colour and a remarkable bouquet, for all its forty years of age, and still with a great deal of fruit and sweetness, yet with the fullness and character to go astonishingly with the oily, salty, smoky fish, and the lemon that we squeezed over it.

Here, it was not so much complement but contrast, and my hosts told me that the Rayne-Vigneau was younger and had retained more sweetness than most of the old Sauternes they had drunk recently with smoked salmon – among them a 1916 Rieussec and a 1914 Yquem – and that it was always old wines that they served in this way.

Apart from Yquem itself, the prestige of which is now so overwhelming that, magnificent as it can be in some years, it is – in my belief – always grossly overpriced and, in other years, sometimes deeply disappointing, the great sweet wines of Sauternes do not receive the attention here that they deserve.

Served very cold with a peach or a pear after dinner, with
crème brûlée or *crème bacchique*,* or by themselves, for their
own sweet sake, in tulip-shaped claret glasses, but only one-
third or one-quarter full, they are surpassed only by the
noblest late-gathered hocks, and the hocks are vastly dearer –
more so even than the greatest years of Yquem, though I
think they deserve to be. And, when very old, they retain
great character, and can be drunk with savoury dishes, as I
learned over the smoked salmon.

Yet such is the present prejudice against sweet wines, arising
from unreasoning snobbery – how can one drink a dry wine
with, or after, fruit? – that no English wine-merchant I know
of lists more than three or four of the great first growths and,
apart from the now overpriced Yquem, those that are listed
are cheaper than they have a right to be: at the end of 1966
it was possible to buy the London-bottled 1962 Château
Coutet and Château Rieussec, both first growths, at 18s. 6d.
and 15s. 6d. a bottle respectively. Unlike the dry white wines,
these are wines to be laid down, for their sweetness gives them
great staying power, and I recommend buying them in half-
bottles for, drunk as dessert wines, they go a long way, and a
half-bottle with fruit after dinner is not too little for four
people.

So much greater is the demand, these days, for dry white
wines than for sweet that some of the great sweet-wine
châteaux of the Sauternais – Filhot, Lafaurie-Peyraguey and

---

* Two superb, and very simple, puddings: *crème brûlée*, in spite of its name,
is a confection that is said to have originated in Scotland and to have reached
civilized parts by way of the kitchen of a Cambridge college – Trinity? – to
which a Scottish nobleman's undergraduate son had given the receipt. My wife
says that the best recipe for it is in Mr Robin McDouall's cookery book. *Crème
bacchique*, or Bacchus's Delight, is no more than a baked custard of Sauternes,
egg-yolks, not much sugar and, if you insist, a pinch of cinnamon. See *Tante
Marie*.

Yquem itself among them – are devoting some of their space, time and effort to dry wines, but I find them coarser than I like a dry white wine to be. Perhaps a wider use of the riesling grape in these parts, and its acceptance by the various official bodies concerned with *appellation* as a "noble" grape for the Bordelais, as it is for Alsace, will lead to greater delicacy.

The Graves, too, as well as the Sauternais, is now producing a lighter, drier wine than the typical "medium-dry" Graves – the so-called Château La Tour Alain is named after the late Allan Sichel (who also had a hand in persuading Château Filhot to produce a dry wine) and who suggested to an eminent grower of Graves rather earlier picking than usual – the grapes fully ripe, of course, but not lusciously so, and concentration on the sauvignon rather than the semillon grape, as it ripens more slowly and thus does not become too ripe if picking has to be prolonged. Then, the completest possible fermentation so that there is no residual sugar. The result is crisper and more refreshing than one usually finds in white Bordeaux and, because of a more settled climate, capable of being produced more cheaply than wines of comparable quality from Burgundy or the Rhine. I still prefer, myself, a fine German wine, but as good a one would certainly be dearer.

Among the dry white wines, I wish I knew more about those of Burgundy – but then I know little of its red wines, either. There seem to me to be few types of wine where the differences in quality, character and subtlety between the cheap and the dear are greater: I have had white burgundies with those who know about them, and notably under my colleague Mr Edmund Penning-Rowsell's roof, that showed more firmness and body than one finds in the Germans and Alsatians that are my favourites among white wines, and yet far greater charm and delicacy than any of the white Bordeaux, but I find in oyster bars and restaurants – even in the tasting-rooms of distinguished shippers, whose wines I know to be above suspicion and beyond reproach – Chablis and Pouilly-Fuissé with no character or style at all. Cheap white burgundy, however authentic as to its origin, seems to me to taste of nothing.

The same cannot be said of any of the wines made from the remarkable, ubiquitous riesling grape, which is grown all over the world, from Australia to Brazil and from the South Tyrol to South Africa. There is more than one kind of riesling: in Italy, for instance, distinction is made between the riesling Renano – Rhine riesling – and the riesling Italico – Italian riesling – but I assume that they are all closely related. Certainly, they all seem to me to share a close family resemblance.

Particularly, though, wherever the German language is, or has been, spoken – whether by the people of the place, as in Alsace, Austria, and Germany itself, or by the proconsuls and bureaucrats who ruled outlying provinces of the Austro-Hungarian Empire for the Hapsburgs – there grows the riesling grape, Nowhere, I suppose, more widely and nowhere, certainly, with greater commercial success than in Slovenia, once part of the province of the Empire known as Styria, now the north-westernmost republic of the federal state of Yugoslavia.

It is the grape that put Yugoslavia on the wine map of the world. Who, before the war, had ever heard of Yugoslav riesling? Now, who has not? Britain, I am told, imports something like half a million gallons of Yugoslav wine a year, and one out of every twenty-five bottles of table wine drunk in this country is a bottle of Yugoslav riesling. If the propor-

71

tion were to *white* table wines, the figure would be even more remarkable.

Heavier and coarser than the comparable German and Alsatian wines, probably because they get more sunshine – heavier, too, than those of Hungary and the Alto-Adige, which may get as much sunshine but probably make up for this by the greater altitude of the vineyards – and also because they are blended, not single-vineyard, wines, nevertheless they have much of the riesling fragrance and something, too, though not so much as the rieslings of Germany and Alsace, of its characteristic "balance" between fruitiness and acidity. They are better value – largely, I suppose, because they are made in and marketed by efficient co-operatives with modern machinery – than the cheapest German and Alsatian rieslings, though not in the same class as the finest, and they have done much to popularize their rivals and their betters: I hope that the German and the Alsatian growers – to say nothing of those of Hungary and the rest – are grateful to them.

It seems strange now that fewer than fifty years ago, in the 1920s, the wines of Alsace were as unfamiliar to the wine-drinkers of Britain and, indeed, of France as were those of Yugoslavia immediately after the war, in the 1940s: George Saintsbury, whose *Notes on a Cellar-Book* came out in 1920, wrote about Picardan and Ampurdam, Tent and La Frette, with never a word for the wine of Alsace which, well within a half-century, was being summed up by an equally distinguished amateur as, "one of the most delicate and fragrant wines that exist", a judgment capped by another's opinion of the Alsatian gewürztraminer as, at its best, "one of the really great wines of the world".

Before 1870, the peasant-farmers of Alsace went in for quantity, not quality, and their wines were overshadowed by those of other parts of France. From 1870 to 1918, Alsace was under German rule, and its wines used for blending with those of Germany. It was not until 1919 that the Alsatian growers were able to go in for quality and – an even longer and an even harder job – for persuading the outside world that they were succeeding.

One thing they did, both to show good faith and to make their wines more easily recognizable (and their names more pronounceable) was to name their wines after the grapes they are made from, and eventually we learned to look to the sylvaner for lightness, the riesling for crispness, the pinot gris, or Alsatian tokay, for fullness and fruit, the traminer – and its spicier, fuller variant, the gewürztraminer – for bouquet and body.

Alsatian wines never taste as sweet as they smell; they are almost invariably drier than their German cousins. Yet there are late-gathered wines that have not only the fragrance but the richness to drink with fruit, even though they are acid enough not to be cloying. A Schlumberger pinot gris (or tokay) 1958 that I drank at a Wine and Food Society dinner in 1961 or thereabouts still lives in my memory as the perfect partner for the dish it accompanied – a confection of peaches and cream: the pinot gris, when late-gathered, makes a wine that Mr Edward Hyams has described as, "a full, smooth, opulent yet sufficiently acid wine of outstanding fruity- fragrance". Nothing like so sweet as a Sauternes or a trockenbeerenauslese hock, and yet a superb dessert wine.

These hugely full and fragrant white wines are, in fact, the obvious answer for those who like to drink wine with fruit, but find the classic white dessert wines too sweet; at the same time, a really big and heavily scented Alsatian gewürztraminer will go with *foie gras* or the richest lobster dishes, where lesser wines would seem thin and acid. In the same sort of way, one of the more important Alsatian rieslings – a Réserve

73

Spéciale, say, or a Grande Réserve, which are what the Germans would call *spätlese* and *auslese*, late-gathered and specially picked, respectively – will not be abashed in the face of a really full-flavoured meat dish.

With grilled fish, though, or, in Alsace itself, with locally caught trout, dressed only with melted butter, I would choose one of the younger and lighter rieslings, or even a sylvaner – sylvaner is a wine with no very great pretensions, but deliciously refreshing when drunk cool: a wine that drinks itself, as the locals say. I am very fond of the sylvaner as an aperitif, and in Alsace they have a custom I have not come across elsewhere, of not only drinking it before the meal, but going back to it after each course as a *rince-gueule* – a mouth-wash – before serving the richer food and richer wine of the next. Better than Vichy.

Dr Fritz Hallgarten has recorded a memorable Alsatian meal that was preceded by a young sylvaner, and then began with onion soup. Then pike and an older riesling, and a sip of the sylvaner, and then the main course – ham *en croûte* – with a pinot gris, or Alsatian tokay, and again a sip of the sylvaner, followed by cheeses from the Vosges accompanied by a gewürztraminer, followed by the sylvaner yet again before going on to sweetmeats, and back to the tokay that had been served with the ham. A meal notable for two things – not only for the use as a sort of sorbet between the courses of the wine that had been served as the aperitif, but where else in the world would you find a wine to go both with ham *en croûte* and with sweetmeats, as did that tokay d'Alsace?

Though I might have preferred, myself, with the pudding, the 1959 traminer *beerenauslese* that I drank with Jean Hugel and his wife in the gabled, half-timbered, whole-heartedly window-boxed and picture-postcarded Hansel-and-Gretel

Alsatian town of Riquewihr, where the Hugels have been growers and shippers of wine since 1637. Only 753 bottles of the great dessert wine had been made, picked grape by grape as they withered into sulatana-like sweetness on the vine – a wine with great sweetness and fruit, yet nothing like so lusciously sweet as a German wine of the same type, still less as sweet as a great Sauternes.

We drank it with an apricot-meringue confection of Madame's, and Jean Hugel swirled his glass and held it to his nose, looked reflectively into the middle distance for a moment, and then caught my eye, and gave the sort of shy, proud, half-smile that a father might give to a friend who watched with him as a son made a century at Lord's. Madame intercepted the glance, and turned to me with, "Jean est amoureux de ses vins". No wife could have been prouder of a husband's love-affairs.

Even now, well-known as they have become, the wines of Alsace do not come one's way as often as those of Germany, or as the French classics that are far older-established in the English market, such as claret, burgundy, or champagne. Which may be why I have never had a bad one – I have sometimes been disappointed in a sylvaner's lack of bouquet or, contrariwise, by a traminer's tasting less bewitching than its scent had promised, but I have never known an Alsatian wine seem coarse, or ill-bred. Nor violent, either, though it may be that some day I shall be obliged to put to the test that renowned wine of Wolxheim, which they used to say would break a man's legs under him.

Some people complain of the great wines of Germany that they are "difficult to drink": that the bigger and more important wines are too fruity – too nearly, if not completely, sweet – to drink with cooked dishes. Certainly, the Germans themselves form partnerships of great, flowery wines with salmon, or chines of venison in cream sauce, that are not to the English taste in wine-and-food combinations. And many German wines, certainly, are easier to drink after dinner, for their own sake, than as accompaniments to savoury main courses.

But, faced a few years ago with the problem of entertaining in my own home a *Guide Michelin* inspector, who daily consumed, in the line of duty, the finest dishes and the noblest wines of France, I decided to partner the best that England could do – smoked salmon, saddle of lamb, Stilton and strawberries (and not chosen for the sake of assonance, either) – with first of all a light, crisp, young Mosel; then a Würzburger Stein Sylvaner Auslese that was dry and flinty, yet big enough, as a full white wine can be, to go with roast meat; and with the strawberries a great trockenbeerenauslese hock that had captured a whole Rhineland summer of the scent of blossom and the sweetness of fruit. A host should not say it, but the wines were superb – and a revelation, too, to my French friend, for the French at home never see a fine German wine.

Or know, indeed, some of them, that Germany grows wine at all. I remember staying once at Loudenne, the Gilbey château in the Médoc, when old Madame Gombeau was still alive – widow of the Camille Gombeau who had managed the vineyards long before the First World War.

It was in the 1950s that I met her, when she was eighty or thereabouts, and she recalled how, during the Second World War, a couple of German officers had been billeted on her at Loudenne – "very nice and correct, perfect gentlemen and, do you know, Mr Ray, one of them grew wine! Yes, he was a German, and he grew wine – back home, in Germany.

"And what do you think, Mr Ray?" she went on: "When

he went off to Germany on leave he came back with a bottle of his wine – and it was very drinkable."

The old lady nodded her approval, in a judicious rather than a condescending way, but was unable to keep the recollection of surprise out of her voice. Then she said, "But the remarkable thing was, Mr Ray, that it came in a long, narrow bottle like this, without any shoulders" – and she sketched a hock bottle in the air with her hands – "I don't suppose you've ever seen such a bottle, Mr Ray, but that's the sort of bottle they put German wines in." And it was clear that she had not only never seen or heard of a German wine before the occupation, but had never seen an Alsatian one, either. Indeed, as a true Bordelaise, she may well never have allowed a drop even of burgundy to pass her lips.

It is understandable enough that little German wine should find its way into France: there is little of it, and the best of it is dearer than most comparable French wines, because it is grown with the greatest difficulty, most of it on precipitous hillsides, in a region where the climate is only just suitable for wine-growing, and that not in every district, every year. And then Germany produces only one-thirtieth as much wine as France – about half as much as Greece and a good deal less than California. Yet there are 52,000 different, named German wines: you could drink a different one every week if you lived to be a thousand, and I cannot think of a better way of passing the time.

Any nomination of individual wines, therefore, is madly arbitrary, and if I point out that the three wines I offered to my friend from *Michelin* came from three distinct wine-growing regions – the dry, light aperitif from the Mosel, the wines of which tend to be lighter and drunk younger than those of the Rhine (the Germans talk of "the lords of the Rhine and the ladies of the Mosel": the wines of the Saar and the Ruwer valleys, which are entitled to the name Mosel and the slim, green bottle of the Moselweins, not the slim, brown bottle of the Rhine, are lighter still); the wine with the main course from Franconia, in the flagon-shaped bottle of the region (the *Bocksbeutel*, so-called because it is said to resemble in shape the scrotum of a goat), where the wines are dry and full-flavoured; and the dessert wine from the Rhine itself, and big and fruity – this is not to say that it could not have been done quite differently, serving a drier Rhine wine with the meat, a young Franconian wine beforehand, and a luscious, late-gathered Mosel as dessert.

Ever since Dr Adenauer gave General Eisenhower a much-publicized present of Berncasteler Doktor, there has been a great demand in America for the finest German wines, but the best still come to Britain, where there are still amateurs not only keen enough but rich enough to pay, say, sixteen or seventeen guineas or so a bottle – far more than they will for even the finest Yquem – that Mr Peter Hallgarten told me in 1966 would be the retail price of the 1953 Schloss Vollrads Trockenbeerenauslese or the 1959 Wiltinger Braune Kupp und Hoelle Trockenbeerenauslese Cabinet that he and I tasted one day along with Peter's father, Dr Fritz Hallgarten, and Mr Walter Sichel. The second of these wines I think is one of the most exquisite of the sort I have ever tasted, and I was assured that it would go on getting better still in bottle for another twenty or thirty years, and still be splendid after fifty.

Dr Otto Loeb made a similar claim for the dessert wine he served at a Moselwein luncheon he entertained me to in London in 1965 – the 1959 Serriger Schloss Saarfelser Vogelsang Cabinet Trockenbeerenauslese, and if one exclaims at so jaw-breaking a concatenation of consonants it must be pointed out that my host said, "Mind you: they *could* have got still another word in, if they'd wanted." He sketched a modest nod – he is a small man of even smaller gestures – towards the half-bottle and observed that a German wine is entitled to state on its label not only

the village it comes from: Serriger (from Serrig);

the estate: Schloss Saarfelser (from the Castle of Saarfels);

the vineyard: Vogelsang;

the quality: Cabinet (meaning the sort a grower keeps in his own special cupboard);

and the stage at, and manner in which, the grapes have been gathered: Trockenbeeren (when the berries are so over-ripe as to have dried on the vine), Auslese (individually selected grapes);

but also the variety of grape, so that the label *could* have read: 1959er Serriger Schloss Saarfelser Vogelsang Riesling Cabinet Trockenbeeren-Auslese, save that in wines of this quality it is taken for granted that the grape *must* be the riesling, that being the noblest of German grapes, and so the word is sometimes omitted. Dr Loeb is a notable scholar, not only of German wines in general and of the wines of the Mosel and its tributaries in particular, but also of music (he created the famous Glyndebourne wine list, and spends his holidays there and at the Aldeburgh Festival).

An already distinguished London wine trade acquired even greater distinction in the 1930s, when Hitler drove to these shores men such as the Nassauers, Fritz Hallgarten, Walter Sichel, the late Alfred Langenbach and Otto Loeb. It is nice to know that in Otto's case his native city of Trier made what amends it could by naming a street after his equally eminent father, and by sending its mayor specially to London to invite Otto to accept one of the city's twelve "seals of honour". I have heard it said that if it is known he is visiting the theatre at Trier the performance begins only when the signal is given that he is in his seat. I would wish Covent Garden to do no less, though it might embarrass so modest a man.

On this occasion, Otto had provided a 1958 Maximin Grünhauser Herrenberg as an aperitif – a light, balanced wine that had taken three years, Otto told me, to lose its initial acidity (the Saar wines are notably light and crisp), and was now charmingly refreshing as the beginning to a summer luncheon; a 1959 Trierer Augenscheiner Stübchen Feine Auslese with the lobster – a golden wine from the sandstone slopes opposite Trier, and softer than its fellow-Mosels, which grow on slate: full and fruity, with a spicy smell and a hint of sweetness, yet dry enough for the fish, and without a whisper of coarseness.

With the strawberries, the climax – the first trocken-beerenauslese to be made in the Saar since 1937, for it is only once in twenty years or so that there is enough sunshine in that northern valley for the grapes to burst with ripeness, suffer the *edelfaule*, or "noble rot" – the same *pourriture noble* that makes the great sweet wines of Sauternes – and dry into the withered capsules of sweetness that become the greatest dessert wines in the world.

For I rank a great German trockenbeerenauslese higher than the greatest Sauternes – a wine such as this higher even than a Yquem of a great vintage – because however lusciously rich and honey-sweet it is, there is always a balancing acidity that makes it less cloying and more subtle than the French wine. It gives remarkable staying-power, too: Otto Loeb thought that this 1959 was only just ready for drinking, and would last for another twenty years and more.

We swirled it in our glasses, and found it so hard to dis-entangle the sunshiny colour and the apple-blossom fragrance from the honeyish, grapy sweetness and the crisp, almost lemony acidity in the mouth that we might have been drinking sunshine and listening to apple-blossom. Here was that famous summer of 1959 in a glass.

We had congratulated ourselves that the growers of this nectar – a Catholic hospice of Trier, doing an unquestionably Christian work – had been thoughtful enough to bottle it in half-bottles as well as in bottles, for these rich dessert wines go a long way. Now I was not so sure: had it been dinner we were eating, and not luncheon, I could have gone on drinking it slowly through the evening, thinking pious thoughts about the good men of Trier – about those who had grown the wine, and about him who was drinking it with me. I heard once of an American visitor to these shores who, on tasting Oxford marmalade for the first time, exclaimed, "There *is* a God!" I was pretty near to getting religion myself, and with better cause.

But I recalled, just in time, that as many of the greatest German wines come from properties owned and managed by various states of the Federal Republic – Rheinhesse, Rheinpfalz and Bavaria among them – as from monasteries and hospices. Indeed, if I were to find myself leader of the Labour Party I would buy up as many bottles as I could and distribute them as widely as possible: I cannot think of a better argument for nationalization.

5 · In the Pink

"Not even a nod in the direction of rosé, that wine of compromise," was a reviewer's comment on a piece I wrote for one of the annual issues of *The Compleat Imbiber*, on what wines to drink with what dishes. I must confess that the omission was due not at all to any strong-minded disapproval of compromises but to sheer negligence: rosé had slipped my mind.

I cannot think why – I suppose I must have drunk and enjoyed as much rosé as most people in my time – unless it is that no dish specifically demands rosé, as fish, for instance, calls for a dry white wine, and the article under notice was about particular wines for particular dishes. In the world of wine, rosé is a jack of all trades, master of none.

Pink wines look pretty, are most pleasing when they are young, and need not be taken too seriously. There are delightful young things of whom one could say much the same: these wines, like those girls, are made to be flirted with. So rosé is the wine for a picnic, or for a buffet luncheon, which to my mind ought to be a sort of indoor picnic, at which great clarets and fine hocks would be overdoing it: one cannot drink a serious wine standing up. Rosé is the wine that one chooses for lightness in the mouth and for pleasure to the eye.

All – or virtually all – grape-juice is colourless, and wine derives its colour from the contact of the juice with the skins of the grapes from which it has been pressed: white wine is made by taking the juice away immediately, and red wine by leaving juice and skins together during fermentation. Some of the cheaper rosés are made by mixing red wine and white, or even by colouring white wine with cochineal, but the true rosé is made by running the juice off the skins of black grapes after a longer contact than a white wine would have, but before fermentation. This means that not only does the wine derive less colour than a red wine would, but less body, flavour and staying power, from pips and skins: rosé should be light and fresh, drunk young and served cool.

What it does not mean is that rosé wines are necessarily less heady. Alcohol comes from the sugar in the juice, and white and pink wines can be just as strong, alcoholically, as the fullest-flavoured reds. So much so, indeed, that Tavel rosé, for instance, which comes from the Châteauneuf du Pape country, hailed by one great authority, Morton Shand, as among the most delightful of wines – "beautifully clean to the palate, in colour a joy to the eye, dry and yet *fruité*, it has just the right degree of flavour and vinosity" – has been condemned by an equally distinguished connoisseur, Mr Edward Hyams, as "quarrelsome". Which can, of course, be said of any wine drunk perhaps too eagerly, under a hot sun, or in the wrong company.

Both bigwigs were right: what makes Tavel more reliable in quality than many rosés that come to this country is that it "travels" well, and what makes it travel well is a relatively high alcoholic content for a light table wine (it is the lightest and least alcoholic wines that do not "travel"). This is also why Tavel is the only rosé that keeps well: "after a few years' keeping", said Shand, "it is a wine without a fault." But these very qualities, of reliability and of staying power, derive from those that make it less suitable for sun-baked luncheons out of doors than some of the lighter, less distinguished pinks from farther north – from the Loire valley, for instance, where some of the pink Anjou and Saumur wines are truly delicious, made from the same grapes as the finest clarets, with a light, fresh fragrance, and an enchanting whisper of fruit.

Tavel, then, for dull days indoors when, being such a pretty pink, I think it should be decanted for buffet luncheons into clear glass jugs or carafes. Better still, as it ought to be served and kept cold, in one of those Italian wicker-covered *fiaschi* that have a compartment for ice, or one of those German silver-mounted jugs with a detachable ice-cylinder.

There are those, whose taste and opinions I respect, who have no objection to drinking a well-chilled rosé with cold lobster, salmon, or – my own favourite of all cold-buffet dishes – dressed crab. Personally, though, I drink only white wine with fish, even with those – red mullet, salmon and lamprey – that the pundits say will go well with red wine. Not because I am pedantic or puritanical in these matters, but because all fish, in my mouth – and I can speak of no other – gives any red or even any pink wine a taste as of brass filings. (Mr. Walter James, the Australian wine-grower and gourmet, wrote of Tavel that it has, "a hard, metallic taste": I am sure he must have drunk it with fish.) The only exception that I can think of to this rule is the pink Veuve Clicquot I have already mentioned. But perhaps pink champagne is different.

But then all taste in wine is highly subjective, which is why, no doubt, my own choice among rosés is not the aristocratic Tavel, with its true, clear colour, nor one of the charmers from the Loire, but one of those cheaper, less good-looking, no doubt less nice-tasting *pelure d'oignon* wines from the Midi, so-called because their colour is the thin, translucent tawny of onion-skin, and not a true pink. And all because one of them is the wine of the house at a little *bistro* in Paris that I have been going to since the Liberation, when a bottle was planted firmly on my table, and I tasted it for the first time – a wine, therefore, that for all sorts of nostalgic reasons I have drunk at every meal I have had there in the more than twenty years since, with roast chicken, with beef bourguignon, with kidneys in red wine: with everything, in fact, save fish.

It is a wine that I have never bought and never served in England, though various wine-merchants list one. It might be worth trying at a buffet luncheon, though much would depend on where it came from in the first place, and whom it was bought from. It can be rough stuff, and there is always the danger that it might turn out to be like that rosé that the late A. J. Liebling of the *New Yorker*, a fellow war correspondent of mine, was once given at a grand house in Paris, "in an Art Nouveau bottle with a label that was a triumph of lithography; it had spires and monks and troubadours and blondes in wimples on it, and the name of the *cru* was spelled out in letters with Gothic curlicues and pennons".

"What a madly gay little wine, my dear!" said host to hostess – repressing, according to Liebling, but not soon enough, a grimace of pain.

"One would say a Tavel of a good year," cried Liebling himself, adding under his breath, "if one were a complete bloody fool."

The one at my *bistro* is probably no better, and yet when I drink it there it is delicious – which is why I have never tried to drink it at home. Nor can I remember ever having ordered a rosé of any sort in any English restaurant – unlike the friend of mine, home from abroad, who was served with one in London which, he said, looked and tasted like inferior port, watered down. That was what he told the waitress when he complained about it. "Oh, no sir," she replied: "I don't think there could be any mistake of *that* sort. We don't make it ourselves: it comes already bottled from Rosé."

A former colleague of mine, now deceased – Aidan Philip, who used to write erudite cookery articles in *The Observer* under the name "Syllabub" – once devised a menu for a young woman wishing to precipitate a proposal: mulligatawny soup, trout in aspic, new potatoes and salad, strawberry-orange fool and one good cheese, adding that, "a good but safe wine is advisable. A vin rosé meets the case, but it should be a Tavel or a very dry one from Provence". I think nothing at all of pink Provençal wines, and I doubt very much whether Tavel is the right choice in the circumstances save that, as I have indicated, it is stronger than it looks, which may be what is needed. After all, given the right frame of mind, anything will do. When Dick Swiveller bade Little Nell's brother, "fan the sinking flame of hilarity with the wing of friendship; pass the rosy", the rosy was a jug of cold gin and water.

6 · *The Wine when it is Red*

When I am asked, as I sometimes am, what is the bottle of wine I have most enjoyed, I have to answer that it was probably some anonymous Italian *fiasco* that I drank one star-lit Tyrrhenian night under a vine-covered arbour, while a Neapolitan fiddler played "Come Back to Sorrento" over the veal cutlet of the young woman I had designs on, and all the world was twenty years younger. Or, now I come to think of it, the bottle of cheap and dubious St Emilion that was all that the pub across the road had to offer when my wife and I had our first restaurant meal together after our son was born – a meal that my wife had insisted should be at Maurer's in Greek Street (which in those days was unlicensed, so that you had to send out for wine) because she wanted huge helpings of beef goulash and red cabbage after the pallid hospital food.

For not only is taste in wine as subjective as taste in women, but its enjoyment depends more on circumstances than does that of almost any other pleasure:

Oh, better no doubt is a dinner of herbs,
When season'd by love, which no rancour disturbs,
And sweeten'd by all that is sweetest in life
Than turbot, bisque, ortolans, eaten in strife!

Better Moroccan red with one's best friend than Mouton '53 at the hands of an editor who has asked you to dinner to break it gently that he is giving you the sack.

I think, though, that over the years, fond as I am of the light wines of Alsace and the Mosel, I have derived more pleasure from red wines than from white. Indeed, I have often felt a meal to be incomplete, even though an exquisite white wine has accompanied a main course of fish, if I have not finished with at any rate a mouthful of even a very modest red with some cheese. And, at least in recent years, claret has meant more to me than burgundy.

This represents a change, or a development, of taste: when I was young, I preferred burgundy. When I was middle-aged, indeed. As recently as 1953, though I was already a claret convert, I was still fighting something of a rearguard action, and when I drove to Italy that summer with my bride, I insisted on going by Route Nationale 74, because we had introductions to one of the great shippers of burgundy, and I wanted to show my wife, a dedicated claret-lover if ever there was one, that there was merit in a great burgundy, too: I had great hopes of a La Romanée-Conti 1934 that had been promised us by our friends.

We stood in their cellar, in a tiny tasting-room, and the cellarman glided in with the bottle in his hands, as though he were bearing a baby to the font. But the cellar was very deep; the tasting-room was very small; the smell of wine was strong; and my wife – tired from hours in an open car under the hot sun – had a sudden attack of claustrophobia. She dashed for the stairs just as the cellarman entered: I looked in agony from the bottle coming in to my bride going out – and I went out, too. Never let it be forgotten that, between bride and bottle, I chose bride. Just.

Now, although I am sometimes treated to great bottles by good friends who are burgundy-lovers, and am suitably impressed, I find good claret more subtle and more delicate, with what to me seems a better balance between acidity and fruit, than even the best burgundies, which I often find too bland, too unctuous, even. But all this, as I have said, is subjective: I do not seek to say that claret is better than burgundy, only that it is different, and that the difference is such as to make it claret that is more to my taste.

Nor, indeed, does it mean that I can always unhesitatingly pronounce that this wine, tasted blind, is claret, and that one burgundy – only that it is claret that appeals to me more, when it is at its most characteristic. Not every wine runs true to form: there are clarets that approximate to burgundy in style, and burgundies that are lighter and more delicate than one expects. I have heard the late Allan Sichel say that he has confused the two types of wine more than once (this can happen to even the most experienced taster, especially when he is tired), and Mr Denzil Batchelor has recorded that he once asked Mr Harry Waugh, of Harveys and Latour, and a legendary character in the trade for his skill and judgment as a taster, whether he had ever mistaken a burgundy for a claret, and received the rueful answer, "Not since luncheon."

That wine is a living thing is a cliché that we certainly use too much, and perhaps use too indiscriminately, but it is true that wine matures, mellows and declines, and that it can be disturbed by travel and by abrupt changes of temperature. It is also true that wine, like a human being, can have an off day, and can behave out of character. Also, it can suffer by comparison, so that it may seem not only to be poorly, but to be sulking. It was Mr Harry Waugh again, with whom, early in 1965, and with two other friends, both knowledgeable about claret, that I dined to discuss and compare the three first-growth Médocs – the Latour, the Lafite and the Margaux – of 1953. I was absolutely certain beforehand that the Lafite would "show" the best: to me, on its general achievement in recent years, Lafite is the greatest red wine in the world, and I had drunk the 1953 at a friend's house only a few weeks before, and had found it then, as I still think it, one of the most delicious clarets I have drunk in my life. My fellow-diners were of the same mind: they shared my regard for Lafite and had heard wonders of the 1953; we all expected the Latour to be backward, for it tends to be a hard wine, frequently unsurpassed in off years, but stubborn, and slower in reaching its best than the other first growths in good ones; and in recent years Margaux has not enjoyed quite so consistent a reputation as the other first growths (though its 1947 was famous). All three bottles came from Harveys' cellars, and were handled and decanted in exactly the same way.

Yet this particular bottle of the Lafite was a disappointment: it seemed thin and past its best compared with the other two, though I could not believe that the wine I had so enjoyed only a few weeks before could have faded so quickly, and an old friend drank a bottle of the same a couple of days later, and thought it not yet up to its best. The Latour, as we expected, was still unyielding, the tannin masking its charms: Mr Waugh thought it needed another four or five years. And this, of course, made the Lafite seem all the more faded, though we noticed that it "grew" in the glass, which does suggest that it was not so much age that was affecting it (in which case it would have faded further, in contact with the air) as simply being a bottle that was out of sorts.

The friend I mention who had another bottle of the same wine a few days later, and found it still on the young side, offered yet another explanation. All first-growth clarets are château-bottled, but bottling at any château has to take second place to activity in the vineyards – pruning or spraying or picking or some desperate measure occasioned by a crisis in the weather – so that sometimes bottling has to be put off, and the wine in one cask may wait for as much as six months longer in wood before bottling than precisely the same wine in another cask. This cannot but affect staying power, and is one of the arguments in favour of London-bottling. Not that the first-growth châteaux permit this, but we have all had, sometimes, a London-bottled wine of one of the other classi-fied clarets that has seemed in better shape than the same wine, same year, château-bottled. There are good bottlers and bad, of course, but the best London (and Bristol and other British) bottlers are superb at the job, and may well be better than the best in France.

What showed up our bottle of the 1953 Lafite, though, was the Margaux: we were all as agreed that this was the best of the three as we had been agreed beforehand in expecting the Lafite to lead the field. It looked a little older than the others, with its deep amber edge, but was full in flavour and in scent, as well as being perfectly balanced, having lost the tannin that was still toughening the Latour, yet retaining the fruity sweetness that the Lafite had lost. And I was delighted, when I got home, to discover a dozen in my cellar that I had for-gotten all about.

Margaux is not the only château for which 1953 has proved a greater year than at first it seemed to promise. I recently asked Mr Ronald Barton, who lives at Langoa-Barton in the Médoc, where he has been growing Langoa and Léoville-Barton since 1924, what was the best wine he had ever made. He thought for a moment of the 1934 Léoville, but then plumped quite positively for the 1953, though he added a rider about the 1948, that delicious year that came upon all except the most far-seeing of us as a delightful surprise, and of which the Léoville-Barton was so particularly good: I remember being hauled off by Mr Edmund Penning-Rowsell, who now writes so brilliantly about wine for *The Financial Times*, to drink the 1948 Léoville-Barton that he had just discovered was still to be had at the dear old, and now alas departed, Trocadero.

Few wines have given me greater pleasure over the years than Léoville-Barton, which I have drunk in France, in England, and in Dublin at both Jammet's and the Gresham, giving myself in Ireland the additional pleasure of drinking a claret grown by an Irishman. The London-bottled 1949 that I bought from J. Lyons and Company's Hop Exchange Cellars as soon as it was listed must have cost me every penny of eight or nine shillings, and how good it was! And I think that the 1953 that its grower was so proud of would have shown up well even against that exquisite Margaux, and shown much more life and body than the particular bottle of Lafite that had so disappointed us.

For Léoville-Barton, with all its subtlety and depth of flavour, is a full, "fat" wine, which always seems to have great reserves of staying power. Much of this "bigness", Mr Barton tells me, is due to the high proportion of old vines on the property – about half of the Léoville-Barton vines are fifty years old. Age in a vine, until it becomes *too* old – perhaps at seventy or so: it depends on the variety as well as on climate and soil – gives body and quality, at the cost of a reduced yield. But part of the character of Léoville-Barton comes from the soil itself. The Léoville-Barton vineyard meets at various points, but does not march with, that of Langoa-Barton: the vines are the same – 70 to 75 per cent Cabernet-Sauvignon; the same *vignerons* tend the vines of both properties; the wines are both made (but never mixed) under the same roof and by the same people; and yet Langoa always comes on a little more quickly, seldom lasts so long and, fine classic claret though it is, never shows the same delicacy and subtlety as the Léoville. At various times over the years the vines on the two properties have been much of an age, so that the only factor not common to both is the soil – and yet Mr Barton told me that even the most expert soil-chemist cannot define the difference: like most of the vineyards of the Médoc, Langoa and Léoville are both of gravel on a subsoil of clay.*

Both are fine clarets, made very carefully by the same dedicated wine-grower, but this, as Mr Barton himself points out, is why, in the famous classification of 1855, based on the relative prices fetched by the various wines on the open market of the time, and still current, Léoville was put in the second of the five classes, Langoa in the third. Though it must be remembered that the classification of the red wines of the Médoc is a sort of Debrett, and lists only the sixty or so noblemen among more than thirty times as many commoners. If

* It will be noticed that although I write of Langoa that it *never* did such-and-such, *always* did thus-and-thus, I use the less positive word "seldom" about its relative staying power compared with that of Léoville. At the annual dinner of the Circle of Wine Writers in 1965, with M. André Simon in the chair, the crowning glory of a particularly distinguished wine-list was the Langoa-Barton 1928. At this dinner, we are the hosts and our guests are all from the trade: as can be imagined, we feel put upon our mettle to find wines that are not only splendid, but out of the ordinary. Our resourceful secretary, Mr Gabor Denes, had discovered at a City wine-merchants, tasted and rapturously approved a few cases of half-bottles of this rare vintage—and what is remarkable is not only that these were half-bottles, which come on more quickly than bottles, but London-bottled at that, which also sometimes means a quicker maturing than the château-bottled. Yet the wine was full, rich, fragrant and magnificently alive, and when M. Simon paid it its due tribute as the noblest of the five fine wines on parade, our guests from the trade were loud in their agreement.

Lafite is a duke, then Beychevelle, a fourth growth, is a viscount, and Cantemerle, a fifth growth, is a baron: Langoa is an earl to Léoville's marquisate. And just as some of our barons, say, are better-bred, or more agreeable companions, or both, than some of our earls, so there are fifth-growth clarets that one may well prefer to thirds, and as no château calls itself second, third, fourth or fifth growth, but simply and proudly, *"grand cru classé,"* there is no very great general pressure behind the changes that are sometimes proposed, usually by one or other of the very few growers who are disgruntled about their rank.

There are nature's gentlemen among the *bourgeois supérieur*, *bourgeois* and *artisan* growths, too – indeed, if we are to pursue the Debrett analogy, there are many that would appear in Burke's Landed Gentry: I have enjoyed consistently good wines from Château Gloria, which is hard by Beychevelle, and from Château Lanessan, the 1960 of which, a light off-vintage, I bought for the Directors' Wine Club, where it was deservedly successful throughout 1965 and early 1966. As I write, I have high hopes of the 1962 Château Villegeorge, classed as a *cru exceptionnel*, which is between the *crus classés* and the *bourgeois supérieurs*. I remember writing of the 1953 Château Angludet, a *bourgeois supérieur*, that it was, "as charming a wine as one can reasonably hope for" – a wine from a château that had been taken in hand by the late Allan Sichel, a part-owner of Château Palmer (which is a third growth) as well as a shipper, and where his son Peter now keeps open house, and makes good wine.

When we last dined together in London, he providing the 1955 Léoville-Barton and I the food, Mr Barton chose Cheddar cheese at the end of the meal in preference to Stilton, which he held to be too pungent a cheese to go with claret. Yet not long afterwards he wrote to tell me that he had taken the same wine and the 1960 as *provision de bord* with him when he went off on a month's motoring in the Pyrenees, and sent me a photograph of one of his picnic meals: bread, sardines and the 1955 Léoville-Barton out of a French Army tin mug.

There is no inconsistency in rejecting a Stilton with a fine claret, and accepting sardines. There is too much nonsense written and talked about what one may do with wine, and what one must not do: the only rule is for everyone to do what pleases him, when it pleases him, and what may disgust a claret-drinker in St James's Street in June may well enchant the same man, over the same claret, in St Jean-de-Luz in July. *Fay ce que voudras.*

Mr Barton's father used to tell him, "Never drink a good wine until it's ten years old," but that was more than forty years ago, and the advice is hardly valid these days even for claret, much of which is being made to mature far faster than it used to do, and is certainly not valid for burgundy.

The economic motives for the change in vinification methods are clear enough: it is to the advantage of everybody in the trade – grower, *négociant*, shipper and wine-merchant – to have his stocks and his money turning over more quickly. Nor is it to the disadvantage of the consumer, whatever some of the older hands may say, and however eagerly they may look for those – inevitably more expensive – burgundies, for instance, that proclaim themselves as being still made by the *méthode ancienne*: if a wine drinks well when it is ready, it seems to me not to matter at all whether it has become ready in five years' time or in ten. Indeed, the consumer, too, if he stocks a sizeable cellar, may well be glad not to have to tie up his capital for too long.

The changes in method consist, mainly, in the modification of three routine treatments in the pre-1945 system of vinification:

1. At the very beginning of the wine-making process, when the grapes are first gathered, it used to be the practice to feed only some of the grapes into the machine that both crushed them and stripped and ejected the stalks. The larger part of the grapes were put straight into the main press without being stripped of their stalks, which contributed tannin and, oddly enough, sugar to the must. (At this stage, practice differs as between Burgundy and Bordeaux: I think it has always been the custom in Bordeaux to remove the stalks.)

2. In the course of fermentation, the skin, or "head" – a crust consisting largely of stalks, skins and pips – was constantly stirred into the liquid beneath.

3. In the drawing-off stage, the *marc*, or residue of pips, skins and stalks that had been separated from the wine by being drawn off from the fermenting vat, used to be pressed again, very thoroughly, and the liquid thus obtained then blended with the wine from the first pressing, to complete the fermentation in cask.

In many vineyards, these stages are either carried out more lightly now than they used to be, or omitted altogether, so that the wine is lighter in tannin and perhaps even in alcohol, and therefore matures more quickly. It is easy to see that there is nothing unnatural or improper about this modification of traditional methods, and yet there are people who talk and write about "modern methods" of expediting maturation as though some interference with natural processes were involved. (Which is not to say that there are not also improper ways of bringing about the same result – only that good growers have no need to stoop to them, and should not be assumed to be doing so.)

Even when they are made by modern methods, there is great staying power in the best wines of the best years, though it is not always easy for even very knowledgeable members of the trade to know which growers use the old methods and which the new. I wonder sometimes whether the time may come when all those who stick to the ancient ways will say as much on their labels.

There are red wines, though, that are made to be drunk young – such wines of the Italian Lakes, for instance, as Bardolino, from the hills on the Verona side of Lake Garda, where it is grown in surroundings of picture-postcard prettiness. It is a fresh red wine, not unlike its cousin, Valpolicella, which comes from the neighbouring valleys, though it is lighter, if anything, both in colour and in substance, and sometimes has the slightest prickle on the tongue. I have a special sentimental regard for it, because it was Max Beerbohm's favourite wine for casual drinking, mid-morning or mid-afternoon. He would drink, and offer, it cool, as is the Italian custom with these fresh young wines, drunk *all' annata* – "of the year", which is to say, within a year of the vintage – and it was always refreshing after the tiresome drive up to the villa on the noisy, dusty, bustling main road above Rapallo. Then, also to be drunk young, are the kind of Chianti that is put, not into the same sort of bottle as claret (these are the Chiantis that age prodigiously) but into a straw-covered *fiasco*; and, above all, Beaujolais.

We usually spend Christmas in a little country hotel in the north of France, and I recall very well the first Christmas dinner we ever had there – the one that decided us to go there every year. It was a dinner served, in fact, as is the French habit, on Christmas Eve, and with echoes of England about it, save that the roast turkey, with chestnut stuffing, was preceded by oysters from Brittany and a grilled white sausage; and *le plum pouding, flambé* in brandy, followed by such varied

97

confections as a Yule log fashioned largely of cream, and macaroons masked with soft coffee-icing, itself succeeded a plateau of some half-a-dozen cheeses that M. *le patron* has regularly despatched to him, a couple of hundred miles at enormous expense by express train, from the best cheese shop in Paris – which is, of course, that of M. Androuët – for the simple and satisfactory reason that they are that much better than he can get from what you and I would regard as the more than adequate local *fromageries*.

The turkey, what is more, had weighed no more than eight pounds or so before it had been sacrificed on the altar of our gluttony, and had been bought from a farmer known to feed his birds on maize, not on the anonymous feeding-stuffs of the mass-producer. It thus had remained moistly, tenderly and recognizably a *bird*, unlike those British factory-fed monsters of twenty pounds or more – beasts rather than birds – that disintegrate dryly in the mouth as though ingeniously modelled from reconstituted Scandinavian soft-woods.

Great God, even the legs were eatable! Whereas most turkeys I have come across should have had their legs thrown away, and the breasts minced, mashed with butter, flavoured with fresh herbs, fashioned into curious shapes, and then thrown after the legs.

But it is of what we drank with this – by English standards – mere nestling of a turkeykin that I would write, for it was here that we deviated at least as widely from the habits of home. The wine-list included various clarets of distinguished enough ancestry and of adequate age, and I was tempted. But fine clarets of good years are easily enough obtained in England – England is a paradise for claret-lovers – whereas my eye had fallen on the more modest end of the list, where I discovered that a speciality of the house was a Beaujolais *de l'année* – a wine made from grapes gathered no more than some fourteen months before, and bottled early in the year in which we were going to drink it. Common enough in Beaujolais itself, and in a few Paris *bistros* that make a thing of young Beaujolais, but infrequent in the part of France in which we found ourselves. And so our long Christmas dinner was very happily accompanied, first by a light Alsatian riesling, with the oysters and the white sausage (made of pork, chicken, milk and herbs) and then, with the turkey and the cheese, by the delicate, refreshing Fleurie, served cool, as the French always serve young Beaujolais, full of fruit and the freshness of youth, a wine to be quaffed rather than sipped at, and that slaked the thirst as well as pleasing the palate.

The only English restaurant I know of that makes a similar speciality of a Beaujolais *de l'année*, and serves the real thing (though I know some that profess to, and serve the wrong thing), is Mr Gerard Harris's admirable establishment. "The Bell," at Aston Clinton, and thus it was that I once began the day there on Beaujolais.

I had been stood a princely birthday dinner there, at which ten of us had discussed the Bollinger 1955 and a 1962 Chablis; compared the 1929 and the 1953 Gruaud-Larose, in magnums, and the Lafaurie-Peyraguey 1949 with the Deidesheimer Hohenmorgen Riesling Beerenauslese 1950; winding up with an 1839 madeira and a 1906 brandy. Where I dined, I slept, and when I appeared for breakfast my host pointed out that as this was the time of day traditionally devoted to tasting in the Beaujolais, where he goes out every year to buy, and where the wine of the year is sampled at breakfasts of the spicy hot sausages of the district, what about our trying his own *vin de l'année*?

Of the wines of the Beaujolais, those of Chiroubles and Fleurie mature more quickly than those of Juliénas and Brouilly (Morgon might reach its best three months later than the earliest), and so it was that after my bacon and eggs (and after finishing what the birthday party had left of the Deidesheimer Hohenmorgen Riesling Beerenauslese 1950 which, at a fiver a bottle, it seemed a pity to waste), it was a bottle of the Chiroubles 1964 that Mr Harris and I cracked – more, of course, as a matter of pure scientific inquiry than in any spirit of self-indulgence, but taking an austere aesthetic pleasure, nevertheless, in its deep youthful purple, and nodding learnedly at each other over its fresh, vivid fruitiness.

It is very much in the French tradition to drink the appropriate sort of Beaujolais in this way, very young; but Mr Harris is English in his feeling that it ought to be served at room temperature, where the French would drink it cool, and is quite emphatic that this is the way to serve the older wines, though he is ready to be persuaded that cellar temperature is perhaps better in the summer for the younger ones. Cool or *chambré*, he recommends the *vin de l'année* to go with rich peasant dishes, as it might be an *entrecôte marchand de vins*, whereas a claret or burgundy or one of the older, more restrained Beaujolais would go better with plainer grills, with duck or with lamb. Best dish of all on his own menu, he said, to go with a true *vin de l'année* – matching English food with French wine – was the steak, kidney and mushroom pie.

As I sipped the Chiroubles 1964 reflectively I indulged my host by trying to imagine that I had just breakfasted on steak, kidney and mushroom pie, to justify the Beaujolais, but the effort was too much. Enough, I thought, that the year was at the spring, the wine of the year fresh in the mouth, and that I had breakfasted on nothing more out of the way than bacon and eggs and the 1950 Deidesheimer Hohenmorgen Riesling Beerenauslese.

Drinking too old what the wine-grower has meant to be

drunk young can have its serious consequences: it has helped, for instance, to give Italian wines a bad or baddish name here, for Chianti made to be drunk young is cheap, and is shipped here, and aged, whereas the Chianti put up in claret bottles for ageing is dearer than the British market likes to pay, and we do not know what a properly matured Italian wine ought to taste like.

More serious still, at the end of 1966, *The Sunday Times* submitted to a committee of the Union Interprofessionel des Vins de Beaujolais, in Villefranche, fourteen bottles sold as Beaujolais by a wide variety of British wine-merchants. The ten judges were asked simply to decide of each wine whether it was a Beaujolais: "yes"; "possible"; "doubtful"; or "no". Six were rated as positively bogus; four were doubtful; four possible; and none was considered to be indisputably the real, undiluted thing. Now I think it likely that some, at least, of the eight judged to be "doubtful" or "possible" were, in fact, genuine Beaujolais that had been shipped too old or kept too long for them to strike men of the Beaujolais itself, used to drinking their own wines young, as being certainly the real thing. It is significant that the definition of "doubtful", laid down before the judging by the local inspector of the Institut National des Appelations d'Origine, was, "wine of an old colour, tired or thin. Or maderized and therefore impossible to judge with any certainty" – maderisation being the process by which a wine that has been too long in bottle takes on a "brown", madeira-like flavour – and in the course of summing-up the same inspector observed that all the wines submitted lacked the freshness associated with Beaujolais, which made me feel that this must have made it difficult for him to be as sure as he said he was that that they had all been "cut", in varying degrees, "with wines of a Mediterranean nature".

This great Beaujolais test, all the less conclusive in that I am

sure that some, at least, of the wines sold as Beaujolais by
British wine-merchants had been sold to them as such in
France, followed the exposure by a brilliant team of *Sunday Times* reporters of a plant in Ipswich where blended,
pasteurized wine sold in France under proprietorial brand
names (in this case, "Valpierre", described and known in
France as a blend of wines from Provence, the Languedoc and
North Africa) was re-blended, and labelled as coming from
districts and regions entitled to *appellations d'origine*, such as
Nuits St Georges, Châteauneuf du Pape and Beaujolais –
appelations to which the wines were not entitled under French
law. These *appellations* are a warranty of origin, controlled by
the Institut National des Appellations d'Origine, which lays
down the variety of grape a wine must come from, the den-
sity and extent of its planting, the way it must be pruned,
sprayed and trained, and the amount per acre that may be
produced.

Since this exposure, the Wine and Spirit Association has
taken steps to consider applying here the restriction on labelling laid down by French law, but it is important to record
that the *Sunday Times* stories, though correct in every word,
and proper to be ventilated in the press (like the same paper's
previous stories about the auction-room rings: as an old
newspaperman myself, I admired both these stories im-
mensely), nevertheless, by their very publication, threw the
whole matter temporarily out of perspective. The wine trade
as a whole in this country is, and always has been, not only
scholarly but honest, and it was ill-served at the time by its
egregious spokesmen's sophistries about Brussels sprouts not
coming from Brussels, so why should Nuits St Georges be
expected to come from Nuits St Georges, thus confirming the
public in its suspicion that the whole trade was both cynical
and corrupt, and had been lying about its wines for years.

In fact, the trade had long been exercised over the problem of *appellation*. Many firms wanted to fall in with French practice. A few resisted it for dubious reasons: it must be remembered that the Wine and Spirit Association represents the whole trade, saint and sinner, not forgetting the producers of British "wines", made in this country out of imported concentrates and pulps, that would not be entitled under French (or, I think, German or Italian) law even to the name of wine, which is defined in France as, "exclusively produced from the fermentation of fresh grapes or the juice of fresh grapes". Some distinguished firms were against it because we have always been able to import the genuine, finest wines more cheaply than they would otherwise be because we have not needed to import with them the official French *appellation* certificates, which have thus been left in the hands of the French grower or shipper to sell with his surplus or inferior wine to his fellow-countrymen, all the more expensively for being accompanied by a certificate to which it is not entitled.

The trade, then, has always found it difficult to speak with one voice. It was years before the *Sunday Times* revelations that I reported and endorsed in *The Observer* Mr Dermot Morrah's proposed voluntary first step towards applying here the French laws of *appellation*, and claimed that its introduction would not only protect the consumer but also strengthen public confidence in the wine trade. "Can the many highly respected firms," I asked then, "possibly object to their integrity being seen to be beyond reproach, and to the few other firms being shown to be less scrupulous?" But nothing was done, and although the Wine and Spirit Trade Association is now, as I write, at the end of 1966, taking steps to put its house in order, the *Sunday Times* stories have shaken confidence in the trade generally, and the many honourable firms are suffering, as a result of their timidity, a loss of face that they had not deserved through any lack of integrity.

It is as well to be clear what the malpractices really were: it was not the same, as was suggested at the time, as selling margarine as butter: it was more like selling New Zealand butter as French, and even more like selling a blend of various cheaper French butters as Normandy. But it was far removed from the adulterations and sheer faking of Regency and Victorian times, when publications with such names as *The Publican's Guide* and *The Licensed Victualler's Director*, openly on sale, gave recipes for making port out of cider, sloes, beetroot and alum, and Mrs Beeton warned her readers that "immense amounts" of champagne were made in England.

The blended, branded wines that had been re-blended and re-labelled are also sold quite properly here under their own names – there are Carafino and the various Nicolas wines, besides the Valpierre I have mentioned – and are perfectly honest, respectable beverage wines, recognized for what they are by the French consumer, who knows that sound wines come from Corsica and North Africa, and has no snobbish objections to drinking them.

I always drink such wines myself with my holiday picnics in France and at luncheon at home. But in this country, although wine-drinking is spreading more and more widely, it still follows the pattern set by the Edwardian and the Victorian well-to-do, who could afford the best, and the classic regional and vineyard names of France and Germany still possess a cachet that is exaggerated or, at any rate, so imperfectly understood as to be extended to the inferior wines produced by the two countries that also produce the finest wines in the world. I have found myself almost having to apologize at my own table for a wine that I knew to be delicious when I told my guest – thinking that he would be interested, not that he would be shocked – that it came from Chile.

Just as there is a new class of wine-drinker, so, too, new people have been coming into the trade, whose anxiety about turnover and profit margins has combined with the new consumer's anxiety about prestige to make misrepresentation more profitable and more practicable than in the past, especially as the abolition of resale price maintenance, admirable though that measure was, led if not to an all-out price war, at least to some bloody local skirmishes.

When new labelling laws are laid down, we shall have more branded, blended wines to choose from, unentitled to a vintage date or a place name, and more wines from the lesser-known individual properties, entitled to a place-name, but not necessarily better wines than those that are not – *appellation* is a warranty of origin, not of quality. And we shall have to pay more for the very best wines than we do now, because at present they are imported without their official certificates.

Meanwhile, we do well to remember that there are far more honest firms in the trade than dishonest and, when buying the cheapest wines, that those, for example, of Central Europe, the Mediterranean basin and Chile often represent better value than those that sail under false colours so as to benefit by the prestige of the greatest wines of France and Germany, which must always, and rightly, be dearer. To remember this, and to back our own tastes, and not be ashamed of them. It is snobbery that gives cupidity its chance.

7 · *More than Milton Can*

I have never met a true wine-lover who does not enjoy a glass of good beer. Even when I have been touring the vineyards of the Mosel, the Saar and the Ruwer with Dr Otto Loeb, one of the most knowledgeable and most civilized of London shippers of the wines of those parts, we have enjoyed each day for luncheon, between a morning and an afternoon tasting of fine wines, with more to come at dinner, some simple German dish, accompanied always by beer – sometimes by one of the various local lagers; sometimes the dark, porter-like Salvator; or even authentic Pilsener imported from Pilsen itself, in Czechoslovakia, which is one of the best of all arguments in favour of East-West trade.

I know little about beer, but enough to deplore the fact that in this country our beers are losing their individual character because brewing is being concentrated into fewer and bigger hands; because of the replacement of draught beer drawn from the wood by "keg" or "container" beer forced by gas out of metal casks; and because of a greater measure of sterilization and pasteurization of bottled beers.

English snobbery, too, prevents its being taken seriously by those who set standards of taste and patterns for behaviour: what hostess would serve beer at a luncheon party? Or can one imagine, for that matter, an official luncheon for foreign dignitaries, even an all-male one, at which any Government department would serve what is, after all, the wine of the country – followed, say, by an old Highland malt as a liqueur, and preceded by whisky and soda as an aperitif? Yet Winston Churchill would have been better advised to do so than to serve, as one is told he did, Liebfraumilch to Dr Adenauer.

I have given beer luncheons myself, offering carefully chosen beers and old whiskies to male and female guests at least as carefully chosen: I think the meals were enjoyed at the time, but I am sure that no guest felt impelled to go and do likewise – I have never heard tell of such. All I seem to have achieved is to have implanted in a dear woman friend of mine an abiding passion for old Highland malt as a liqueur (whereas the kindest thing said about the alternative after-luncheon drink I offered on that occasion, which was Bass's King's Ale, brewed and bottled for the coronation of Edward VII, which I served in liqueur glasses, was that it was like a tired old madeira. My wife said it was more like Parrish's Chemical Food).

And what I remember best of any of this series of luncheons was being asked across the table by Dr Brian Inglis, then at work on his book on Edward VIII's abdication, whether I recalled what were my feelings at the time – it was so difficult, he found, to recapture actually what was in men's minds, thirty years ago.

But I remembered quite clearly in 1965, I said, what had been my feelings in 1936: what a golden opportunity we were missing of setting up a republic. And as I uttered this innocent remark, I could sense the ladies on my either side freezing and bridling, and even my hasty assurance that I had not been thinking of tumbril and stake but only of dignified retirement in Estoril on what I understood to be a comfortable private income did nothing to mollify either, and whereas the handsome lady on my left never thawed at all, I did at least elicit a wintry smile from the lady on my right by saying that my proposal for the presidency was that it should be held in turn, a year at a time, by holders of the Order of Merit, to which – as had providentially flashed through my mind in the course of my flounderings – her husband had just been elevated.

In writing about beer I must declare my interest, for I have from time to time been consulted, and paid fees, by the firm of Bass, Mitchells and Butlers, who brew not only Bass but Worthington. Had it not been for this, indeed, I should have been inclined to write more frequently than I have of their products in the public prints, for I have derived much comfort from them, and am partial to a bottle of the one or the other in the middle of a working morning.

At home, I must admit, I buy and drink the Bass Blue Triangle or the Worthington Green Shield which, like almost all bottled beers these days, have been chilled, filtered and pasteurized so that they can be bottled "bright", with no sediment; can be stored pretty well indefinitely; and stand up to such unskilled storing and handling as mine or, alas, that of most present-day publicans.*

* Made, as I have mentioned, both by the same big group, Bass is rather more highly hopped than Worthington, and slightly more bitter in consequence:

I hardly ever enter public houses – wet and smelly stand-up places, like other public conveniences – but I think kindly of those few that I know are prepared to go to the trouble of looking after the old-fashioned, "naturally-conditioned" or "matured-in-bottle" Bass Red Triangle or Worthington White Shield, which are bottled straight from the maturing tanks, without any of the modern processing methods, so that the fermentation process goes on, maturing the beer in bottle, "right up to the customer's mouth", as Bass's head brewer once proudly put it to me.

The chief difference in production between these beers and those that our grandfathers knew is that nowadays the brewers begin the maturing process in tanks at the brewery instead of sending the beer to the bottlers to be matured in cask in their cellars; the beer is delivered in tanks from which it can be bottled immediately, and then kept in bottle for about a fortnight before being delivered to pubs and other retailers.

This means that the publican or other retailer needs only to allow the beer to "settle" for about four days – there is no need for skilled handling over a longish period, and less chance of the beer falling out of condition. Once the naturally conditioned beer is settled, it stays in good condition for six weeks or so – the bottles stood upright, and cellar- or larder-cool, not in a refrigerator.

These old-fashioned bottled beers need no other special treatment, save that they deserve to be carefully poured out, and there are still those publicans who make a point of doing so. Maturing in bottle means that there is a certain amount of sediment or deposit left – yeasts and other solid residues – which are quite harmless, but which spoil the brilliance and

Worthington is a shade the blander. Scotland and the north favour Bass; London, the south, and the west country prefer Worthington.

clarity of the beer if they are poured into the glass. Standing the bottle upright, after it has been allowed to rest, means that the deposit will have settled at the bottom, and careful pouring will leave it there, as with the deposit in an old claret, say, or the crust of an old vintage port. And, handled as carefully as I suggest, beers such as the Red Triangle and the White Shield (and I do not know of any other firm that still brews beer like these – not on a scale for national distribution, anyway), even if their flavour is not noticeably superior, do give a much livelier feeling in the mouth than others.

For a short time, some four or five years ago, the same firm produced an admirably bitter, mellow and rather strong beer called Bass Gold Triangle, made from selected barley, matured in vat longer than the others, and not so fully pasteurized. It was sold in "nips", about two-thirds the capacity of the usual half-pint bottle, and the brewers meant it for those who, liking beer as a mid-morning or pre-luncheon drink, found the usual bottle, or half-pint of draught, too much and possibly too weak. Many people, it was thought, ordered gin-and-tonic when they would have preferred a smaller quantity of stronger beer – one nip of Gold Triangle was about the length and strength of a large gin and a small tonic.

Somehow, though, it never caught on. Perhaps it was not advertised enough (it seemed hardly to be advertised at all): the British people will eat and drink anything that is advertised enough, whether it is wholesome and palatable or neither – look at the factory-made sausages, commercial ice-"cream", and tinned tomato soup – and Gold Triangle was uncommonly good beer, by any standards. And I am sure that it was sold too cheaply: when it was introduced, I told the chairman of Bass that it ought to be five shillings a nip – that at two shillings it would never sell. Perhaps if he had made it not five shillings but seven-and-sixpence, or half-a-guinea, it would have collared the market now profitably exploited by the importers of the German Löwenbräu – an admirable beer, but no better, to my mind, than the Gold Triangle – which is sold at about three-and-sixpence a bottle over the off-licence counter, at four-and-sixpence and more at the bar, and which advertises itself as, "the world's most exclusive and expensive beer" (whatever the word "exclusive" may mean in an advertisement that solicits custom).

Another great beer that disappeared from the market, as Gold Triangle has done, but that was then granted a reprieve, is Barclay's Russian Imperial Stout, which had been brewed every year, just before Christmas, almost without a break from the late eighteenth century until the directors of Courage and Barclay decided that it was too expensive to make and not in wide enough demand, and stopped brewing it after the brew of 1963. They then decided, though, that they owed something to tradition, and reprieved it in 1966.

Russian Imperial Stout is so called because as long ago as 1795, Catherine the Great, according to one of her contemporaries, "ordered repeatedly very large quantities for her own drinking and that of her Court". Now, as in those days, it is matured for two months in cask, in what the brewery still calls "the Russian cellars", before being given another year in bottle. It is sold in "nip" bottles that hold about one-third of a pint as against the half-pint of a standard beer-bottle – quite enough to be going on with, for Russian Stout is about twice as strong as Guinness, half as strong again as Bass Barley Wine, and the nip is said to pack the same alcoholic punch as four whiskies. They told me at the cellars that nobody has ever floored four at one go, and not shown the effects.

A smooth, rich, velvety depth-charge of a drink – sweet, but with the sweetness only of the malt, for there is no added sugar, and yet with the bitter tang of hops. The last time I visited the Russian cellars was early in 1966 to taste the 1962, which my expert hosts held to be not so great a brew as the 1951, going on to explain what I had never before realized: that slight differences of temperature and humidity during the brewing and the bottling can affect the quality of a fine beer, and that the year's climate can affect the quality of the malt.

This led to a tasting of one or two that had been specially bottled and long matured. First, the 1957, by then nine years old, poured from a pint champagne bottle that had been corked and wired exactly like champagne, and matured lying on its side. (Beer that is crown-corked must stand up; if it has an ordinary cork, it must lie down like wine.) The cork came out with a pop, and the beer frothed creamily into the glass, dark and rich. Smoother still than the 1962, I thought, but it was surpassed by the 1948, which came from a full-size champagne bottle, smelled like burgundy, and drank like liquid silk.

My hosts told me that they could not always be sure that a bottle as old as this would be as good, but that Russian Stout had a great capacity for ageing. In 1796, Farington recorded in his diary that he drank some of the Porter from Thrale's Brewhouse – the same beer – and that "it was specially brewed for the Empress of Russia and would keep seven years". Clearly, it is capable of keeping – and improving – over a much longer period, and I asked whether these champagne bottles of Russian Stout were generally available for the public to lay down like claret. Alas, no, but the ordinary nips keep quite well, especially if the crown corks are covered with ordinary sealing-wax, to make the bottles really airtight.

When I went over to Dublin in the same year to drink

Guinness with Bryan Guinness, I took him a bottle of the 1958 Russian Stout and one of the 1961, and we found the 1958, then eight years old, in better condition, with more life and sparkle, but the Guinness people decided of their distinguished rival that the 1961 had what they described as, "more style and a cleaner finish".

Bryan Guinness is a poet, a playwright and a novelist, but he is also Lord Moyne, vice-chairman of Arthur Guinness, Son & Co. (known to its employees and to many another Dubliner as "Uncle Arthur"), and it was a matter of pride that my own contribution of the rival brews from London should be matched by all that Uncle Arthur had to offer, from a bottle of Guinness Foreign Extra Stout 1947, brought back from New York, to the current Foreign Extra, by way of Guinness Export, the firm's Porter and the Extra, both on draught, to the bottled Guinness that we all know.

Bryan Guinness is sixtyish, scholarly in voice and manner; and in Ireland, where he lives for half the year, he dresses always in Irish tweed. (I saw him wear two different tweed coats at different times that day, at luncheon and at dinner, and he goes to church in what he describes as "a suit of black tweed-flannel", which he says enables him to get the best of both worlds.) He was one of that gifted Oxford generation that included Robert Byron and Harold Acton, celebrated if not in song at any rate in many stories, notably those of Warden Bowra. They were men of highly idiosyncratic taste, so I was not surprised to find him enjoying the 1947 Guinness which I was not the only guest to find long past its best, thin and acid, which Bryan Guinness admitted, while still claiming to enjoy what he described as its "winey" character. (Rather like the old Bass that I have already mentioned as resembling a tired old madeira.)

The Guinness Foreign and the Guinness Export were both

113

superb beers – the Foreign, which now goes to tropical countries only (and no longer to the United States) and is pasteurized when it has reached the peak of condition, being rather drier and crisper than the Export, which seems softer and rounder – burgundy as against claret, so to speak – and goes to the United States and the Continent. Both are half as strong again, alcoholically, as the Guinness we get at home, and would be very expensive here, because of the higher duty. I realized when I tasted them why it is that a friend of mine who lives in Bonn drinks Guinness there, but not when he comes home to England, and why I have long thought that the best bottle of Guinness I have ever drunk was with my steamed clams and stewed New England scallops at that excellent Brooklyn fish restaurant, Lundy's of Sheepshead Bay: these exported Guinnesses are different from the brew we get at home, and while some (like my friend in Bonn) prefer what they are used to, others (like me in Brooklyn) are seduced by the unfamiliar.

A little cheaper is Guinness Porter, which is available in Ireland but not in England – a lighter beer than any of the others. Bryan Guinness drinks it at lunch as being easier to do an afternoon's work on, and this time we had it with the Galway oysters that constituted the luncheon party's first course – bland, smooth and dark, to offset the cold, sharp, salty, lemony oysters, and yet not too heavy a foundation for the courses to come.

With the jugged hare, bottled Guinness Extra, which is what one gets everywhere in the British Isles and, with the bone-marrow on toast, the similarly ubiquitous draught Guinness – two of the noblest of man-made drinks, though I seem to be alone in preferring the bottled to the draught, for the sake of its slight prickle, which I find refreshing. With these two dishes, though, both were admirably chosen – the

slightly fresher bottled Guinness contrasting with the spici-
ness of the hare, the fuller draught beer complementing the
richness of the marrow.

I suppose it is the dark colour and the thick, rich-seeming
creamy head of Guinness that makes it seem a "heavy" drink
for luncheon, but it is rare among beers in containing no
sugar, and I can do an afternoon's work on a greater amount
of Guinness than on many other, lighter-seeming, beers.

It is true that at supper that night, at Bryan Guinness's house
at Knockmaroon, outside Dublin, there was Vieux Château
Certan 1947 – Dublin has a great claret-drinking tradition
rather like that of Edinburgh's – but as a stirrup-cup at home-
going time there was a Guinness mixture of the vice-chairman's own: Guinness Foreign and Guinness Porter, mixed
and matured to his own taste, and deliciously crisp yet full.

This is the poet who began his piece on "Parties" with the
couplet:

> *Here Friendship founders in a sea of friends,*
> *And harsh-lipped Bubbly cannot make amends.*

But, as another poet once observed:

> *Malt does more than Milton can,*
> *To justify God's ways to man …*

and Guinness did much to reconcile me even to a BEA flight
back to London, thus proving, indeed, that

> *… many a peer of England brews*
> *A livelier liquor than the Muse,*

though Lord Moyne, poet and playwright as well as brewer,
is the one peer of England who strikes the happiest balance.

They told me in Dublin that, contrary to popular belief, there
is no difference, in style or in strength, between the Guinness

brewed there and the one brewed at Park Royal, which is Acton way: samples are being tasted all the time at Guinness's headquarters, and neither the brewers nor the chemists can tell the difference.

Nor, in Dublin, is it made with Liffey water, which should ease the mind of anyone who knows what the Liffey smells like, just by the brewery.

An odd circumstance about Guinness is that if you draw a line diagonally across Ireland from north-west to south-east, the north-eastern half drinks more than nine times as much bottled Guinness as draught, and the south-western half drinks nine times as much draught as bottled. It may be because the north-eastern half, which includes Northern Ireland, has more money, and drinks more at home, as well as in the pub. In County Mayo, which is draught-drinking country, the word for half a pint of draught is "bottle", so that the Mayo man who so flies in the face of local tradition as to *want* a bottle has to ask for "a bottle bottle".

Dublin, too, has its conventions, and it was in Mulligan's of Poolbeg Street – Dublin's pubs are known by their proprietors' names, as it might be Tierney's, say, or Madigan's, not, as with us, by the heraldic devices of their ground landlords – that I told my host that I should like half a pint, thank him very much, only to be gently rebuked for the phrase: "Drinking in Dublin", he told me, "is a manly thing, after all, and it isn't so manly now, is it, to be *asking* for a half-pint, though you may decently drink one, and no reflection on your virility, at all.

"But there's a touchiness here that obliges a man to ask, not for a half-pint, but for a 'glass', which is the same thing, but more delicately put, or even for 'a medium', which also means no more than half a pint, save that this time it's a half-pint in a pint glass, and the importance of a medium is that in hard times you might well win a war of nerves with the curate behind the bar over a medium, if only you could keep your hands off it yourself for long enough for him to feel obliged to add just a little more for hospitality's sake."

And I should explain that in Ireland, in this context, a "curate" is a "grocer's curate", which is the proper name for a barman – in the Irish countryside, bars are often parts of grocers' shops. A curate will not accept a drink from you, and is usually, in fact, an abstainer.

This, I suppose, would be the chapter in which to write about cider, if I had ever come across a cider in this country that I thought worth drinking, and also about mead, if I had ever met one that did not seem to me to be an artificially concocted liquid sweetmeat.* When I was very small – but I remember this only very vaguely – my grandfather used to go in both for mead and for perry, a taste for which he may have brought with him from East Prussia, if indeed they were known in those parts, when he came to England in 1860. Where in Manchester he bought them, round about the time of the First World War, I do not know, nor whether they were more naturally produced in those days than they are now: I think they must have been.

I am no stranger to Coca-Cola. I well remember that on a hot summer's day in Manchester in 1936 a friend, long since dead, stood me a well-chilled bottle of it, which I drained to the last drop. (It was the same year that I tried for the first and last time that staple of what hotels nowadays describe as an "English breakfast" – a packeted breakfast food. Not the one

* Since writing this, I have been introduced to Bulmer's No. 7, a still dry cider, sold in half-pint bottles, that is nearer to the fine dry ciders of Normandy than any other English cider I have come across. It is made by complete fermentation of the juice of bitter-sweet varieties of cider apple, so that there is no residual sugar, and matured for twelve months before bottling.

like loofah, the one like crumbled cork bath-mat.) Then again, in 1958, I was offered a paper cup of it by a Middle East Airlines stewardess somewhere in the air between (I think) Beirut and Amman, and I must have swallowed quite a mouthful before my taste buds had telegraphed their warning message to my brain.

So I am conditioned, if not precisely addicted, to it, but I still fail to understand what there is about Coca-Cola that has made it so universally popular that Atlanta millionaires have made their piles – by which I mean their fortunes – out of it. Nor am I moved by what a Coca-Cola man once said it was, the sentimental tears springing to his eyes, that made the drink, "so romantic to so many people" – "maybe that starry-eyed kid who lives next door to you was sitting in a drug-store booth one night, and maybe they were drinking Coke, and maybe while they were drinking that Coke was the first time that girl let that boy put his hand on her leg."

8 · *After Dinner*

When Dr Johnson said that, "he who aspires to be a hero must drink brandy," it was tipsiness he was talking about, not taste. He "spoke with great contempt of claret, as so weak that 'a man drowned by it before it made him drunk'", and his tribute to brandy was that it, "will do soonest for man what drinking *can* do for him".

There are times when this, too, is a merit, but more frequently I echo the doctor's other good word for it, that "the flavour of brandy is most grateful to the palate". And in doing so, it is the brandy of France and, more particularly, of Cognac that is in my mind, and my glass.

True, all countries that grow wine can, and do, make brandy. I have drunk local brandies ranging from very good to simply horrible in Greece and Italy and South Africa. At one of Israel's wineries, having pulled a face over the commercial brandies that it turned out – far too dark, far too artificially flavoured, far too sweet – I have been agreeably surprised by the brandy that the director then took out of a cupboard saying, "Well in that case, perhaps you'd be interested in a brandy I distil just for myself and my friends: it was put in cask a dozen years or so ago, and I've done absolutely nothing to it since – no caramel, no vanilla, no sugar. Just brandy, in oak casks." Very good it was. And a really fine old brandy from Soviet Georgia (it isn't *only* peaches, down in Georgia) was served at our hotel in Kiev during the Macmillan-Selwyn Lloyd visit in 1959. (It was the morning after a night out on it with fellow-journalists that I told my guide-interpreter – a nice but desperately earnest young woman from Moscow University – that no, I *didn't* want to be taken on a tour of a prize-winning collective farm with Mr Macmillan, or even on a visit to the museum of the scientific achievements of the Soviet Socialist Republic of the Ukraine: what I wanted and what, indeed, I proposed to do, was to sit at a café table and watch the girls go by. My guide looked almost tragically reproachful: "Mr Ray," she said, "*Oh*, Mr Ray! You are *very* light-minded.")

Not only other countries than France, but other parts of France than Cognac make brandy: the London firm of G. F. Grant used to ship, and Wolfe's restaurant in Kensington used to serve – perhaps they still do – a light and delicate *fine de la Marne* from Champagne, produced in such small quantities at one distillery in Ay as to be hard to find even in Rheims and Epernay; and there are Armagnacs a great deal more distinguished than one would suppose from the madly picturesque bottles in which they are sometimes offered, fit only to be made into table lamps for tea-shops in the baked-beans-on-toast belts of English cathedral cities.

But the best brandy in the world, indisputably, is that produced in a strictly delimited area, within the *départements* of

Charente and Charente Maritime – the same area that the delicious little Charentais melons come from – distilled from wine *made* in that area, only of the grapes *grown* in that area and, moreover, only of the *types* of grape permitted to its making by the stringent law of France, and permitted by that law – in France and in those countries that honourably choose to observe and obey French law in this respect – the noble name of cognac.

Noble indeed. It is said that throughout the civilized world the two best-known names of French towns are Paris and Cognac, and Morton Shand wrote of a Bishop of Angoulême at a gathering of princes of the Church in Rome who introduced himself as, "Bishop of Engolisma in the Charente", which was greeted with blank stares until he added that this meant that he was also Bishop of Cognac, upon which the scarlet skull caps of Cardinals, "bowed in smiling comprehension, while the whole priestly company burst into a paean of, 'Oh, the splendid, the superb see of Cognac!'".

Yet the town of Cognac itself is small to bear so resounding a fame – as populous as Buxton, say, or Bury St Edmunds: a quiet grey place in a quiet green landscape, under the shallow-pitched roofs of which, sooted with brandy fumes, the colourless spirit distilled from the thin, harsh wine of the region ages into golden maturity in casks of oak from the nearby forests of Limousin and the Tronçais, and only from the edges of the forests, at that.

English, Russian and American oak have all been tried and found unsuitable, as has oak even from other parts of France (and even from too deep within the heart of the Limoges forest itself, where the timber is too close-grained, and splits awkwardly). One will make the maturing cognac too bitter, another too musty, another too astringent. It is from the oak that the brandy – colourless to begin with – takes its golden hue, a touch of sweetness, and the tannin to increase its staying power. It is in the oak that the fiery young spirit ages into its mellow maturity. There is a natural, yet mysterious, affinity, as one writer has put it, between this particular wood, from Limoges and the Tronçais, and this particular brandy, from the immediately adjacent region. Armagnac develops quite differently, and becomes more dark in the black oak of its own forests.

The coopers who make the casks are craftsmen as dedicated as the distillers who tend the traditional pot-stills, and the vignerons who grow the grapes from which the wine is pressed. The staves must be split and shaped by axe, not by saw, lest the oak fibres "bleed" and lose some of their virtue. No nail must be driven into them. Once shaped, the staves must mature in the open air for at least three years, and once made into casks they must be steam-heated and then conditioned by ageing with new brandy – the first brandy to be put into them (one of the commoner types) stays for only a matter of weeks, lest the new wood gives it too much tannin, too much bitterness, and "drowns" its aroma. Then it is taken out, and put into older casks, and the next brandy in the new cask may be left for a year, and so on, the brandies getting older, and the cask itself more mellow.

Cognac matures partly by virtue of the qualities it derives from the oak in which it ages, partly by the very gradual action of evaporation through the pores of the wood, and of the slight and gradual entry of the air through them, playing upon the spirit within. These effects vary according to the climate in which maturation takes place – under a hot sun and in a dry atmosphere, as in Cognac itself, the brandy evaporates more quickly but retains more strength than in a cooler, damper, atmosphere. Thus, cognac landed in London (or Bristol or Liverpool) soon after distillation, and matured in cask under grey English skies becomes, by the time it is bottled, softer, lighter – in colour, alcoholic content and flavour – than the same spirit matured under the bright, hard sunshine of the Charente.

The spirit maturing in the casks is distilled in much the same way as many a less distinguished liqueur. Within a very few months of the vintage, and in any case before the following spring, the thin young wine of the region is taken to the copper boilers, each holding a couple of hundred gallons or so of wine, and boiled over a brick furnace. What especially differentiates the process of distillation here from that of other regions and other brandies is that the apparatus is small and old-fashioned, because no newer type, such as those that distil grain whiskies, is considered – even by the biggest and most progressive firms – to convey into the brandy the most delicate flavours and aromas that the thin wine gives up to the art of the distiller. Distillation is in two stages, each taking about eight or ten hours. The "head" and the "tail" of the distillation are put aside, as being inferior, and have to be redistilled: the "heart" remains.

These slow processes, old-fashioned apparatuses, and highly-developed, inherited individual skills are, by their very nature, expensive. They are typical of, but not entirely peculiar to, the production of cognac, most delicate, subtle and fragrant of brandies. They contribute considerably to its high quality and to its distinctive character. But there are other, and even more indispensable, contributory factors. First of all, the wine that goes into the still. The legally de-limited area of Cognac is divided – also with the force of law – into six parts, which in descending order of the excellence of the brandies they produce are: Grande Champagne, Petite Champagne, Borderies, Fins Bois, Bons Bois and Bois Ordinaires, which lie, very approximately, in concentric circles, with Grande Champagne (in which lie Jarnac and Segonzac) at the centre. The names of the districts Grande Champagne and Petite Champagne (the town of Cognac itself lies where they join) have nothing to do with that part of France, three or four hundred miles to the north-east, whence comes the sparkling wine that is as much the paragon of its own kind as is cognac among brandies. It means simply "open country", whereas the Bois brandies – *fins*, *bons*, and *ordinaires* – come from country that was once thickly wooded.

The brandies of the Grande Champagne, where the soil is thin and chalky, are the most delicate of all, in scent and in their subtleties of taste; those of the Petite Champagne are perhaps, to the most sensitive of palates, a shade less elegant, a shade more full in flavour, because the soil is richer, but the difference is small indeed; the region of the Borderies has more clay, and its brandies have a somewhat richer quality of their own, and age more quickly.

The three districts of the Bois produce very good brandies, but they lack the finesse of those grown in the three innermost regions; they age more quickly; and they have more "body".

Brandies produced from any one of these six districts, or from any combination of them, are entitled to the name of cognac, and this in itself is a patent of nobility. But the finest cognacs of all are those entitled to proclaim themselves proudly on their labels as being not only cognac but "Grande Fine Champagne "(or "Grande Champagne", which is the same thing), or as "Fine Champagne" cognac, and the law requires that these shall be solely from the innermost Grande Champagne district in the first case and, in the second, a blend of not less than 50 per cent of Grande Champagne, with the remainder of the blend Petite Champagne and no other. (Many famous distillers maintain that a Fine Champagne is better-balanced between delicacy and flavour, and matures more consistently, than an unblended Grande Champagne. But both are at the very top of the cognac tree, and any discussion of their respective merits is on a level almost metaphysically high.)

This does not mean that the Borderies and the Bois produce poor brandies – it is simply that they are not so delicate as, and that they mature more quickly than, those of the two Champagne districts. I have tasted well-matured, unblended Borderies and Fins Bois that were splendid cognacs by any standards. And many very sound cognacs indeed, marketed under brand names by the most distinguished houses, are blends that combine the delicacy of the Grande and the Petite Champagnes, the greater body and blandness of the Borderies, and the vigour and earthy flavour of the Bois.

Brandy, like wine, matures in wood; unlike wine it does not mature in bottle: once a cognac has been bottled, it stays as it is. A 1900 cognac bottled in 1930 is still a thirty-year-old cognac in 1967: if it was a good cognac in 1930 it is a good cognac now (unless the cork has deteriorated, or it has been badly stored); if it was a poor cognac in 1930, the thirty-odd years in bottle will have done nothing to improve it.

But, whilst in wood, cognacs from different districts or of different vintages will mature in different ways and at different rates and, to make life even more difficult for the producers of cognac, cognacs of the *same* vintage and from the *same* district will mature differently in different casks.

There is no such thing to be obtained commercially as a completely "single", which is to say an unblended cognac, of one year and from one vineyard, though such things exist, of course, in the distillers' stocks. Nor would it necessarily be a great gastronomic experience to meet one. The small growers of the Charente sell their wines to the distillers – most of them are extremely big commercial firms – and the art of the distiller is to blend vintages, vineyards and regions so as to produce, as a harmonious whole, a perfectly balanced cognac. True, there are still reputedly single vintage years to be had, not of a single vineyard – the vineyards of the region are too small – but of a single district. They are to be found especially in the great Paris restaurants, such as the 1906 Grande Fine Champagne that will cost you 22 francs for an after-dinner glass at Lasserre, or at a few of the great English wine-merchants, such as the Exshaw Borderies 1928 that Harveys used to sell at their Pall Mall shop, at well over £4 a bottle.

But cognacs such as these are becoming fewer, and will eventually disappear, because in 1962 the French Government laid it down that it would no longer officially certify the age of any brandy beyond five years – and what is not officially certified may not, in France, appear on a label. Brandy in cask evaporates, up to as much as 4 per cent in a year – though this percentage diminishes year by year – and so a cask has to be "refreshed" or topped up. It is virtually impossible to prove that any one cask has been topped up only from another cask of the same age and the same provenance (nor would this necessarily be the best way to produce the best cognac) and the Government nowadays will only permit a vintage label if the cognac could be *proved* to be 100 per cent of that vintage.

Not that age is all-important. Cognac improves and matures in wood, but not indefinitely – about seventy years is generally regarded now as the optimum, though this can only be a generality because, as already pointed out, no two casks mature at the same pace or in the same way.

After a time, cognac in wood becomes "woody" and harsh, or fades into insipidity. This is why claims to very great age must be regarded with caution, if not scepticism. A bottle with such a date, say, as 1815 *may* be from a cask begun in that year, and refreshed each year with younger cognac of similar style and quality: by now, there would be nothing left of the original 1815 but the date and the cask. Such a brandy might be very good, but cognac from a cask in 1815 and refreshed from other casks *of the same age* would almost certainly be disagreeable, if not actually nasty, and the price would have been brought to some astronomical number of francs: my old friend Mr Vyvyan Holland, a great wine-lover and brandy-bibber, has worked out that eight casks of 1830 cognac once owned by a Paris wine-merchant had dwindled by 1920, in the course of evaporation and mutual topping, to one cask that was worth £250 a bottle.

On the other hand, of course, a restaurant may have stocks of genuine old *bottled* brandies, such as Lasserre in Paris bought from the old Chapon Fin in Bordeaux, going back to an 1820 Fine Champagne at 60 francs a glass. If carefully looked after, in an even temperature, and kept standing up, so that the spirit does not dry out the cork and shrink it, letting air in, these will be as good as when they were bottled – certainly no better, perhaps no worse. At the Tour d'Argent, I have tasted the 1914, the 1875 and the 1870, and there was no doubt in my mind that the 1914 was the best of the three – a superb cognac – and that the 1870 was finer than the 1875, which tasted, it is true, better than it smelled, but reeked coarsely of wood. There, then, the youngest of the three was the best, yet the oldest was better than one five years its junior: there can be no rule of thumb, and relative prices depend not so much on relative quality as on the length of time that capital has been tied up in each bottle: the best of the three was the cheapest.

What, then, of "Napoleon" brandy? The answer is implicit in what has gone before. There can be no such thing as a drinkable cognac now in cask that is 100 per cent of the first

Napoleon's time. Even of the third Napoleon's, it is more than unlikely. Yet every few months the hoary old legend of "Napoleon brandy" obtrudes itself on to my attention, as it does, I suppose, to that of every wine-writer. Some reader writes or telephones that he has a bottle of Napoleon brandy of unquestionable authenticity – why, there to prove it is the embossed "N" on the bottle, or the date 1811 on the label! – and he is told that it is worth an enormous sum: please can I tell him where to sell it?

Whenever one of the correspondents of a popular paper reports – as I remember happening – that the local cinema has one on view in its foyer, labelled as being worth £1,000 and locked in the safe every night or, as happened a Christmas or so ago, the BBC interviews a wine merchant (since deceased) who claimed to have sold four bottles at £1,000 apiece, and to be negotiating the sale of a fifth, the letters and the telephone-calls redouble.

Mr Tom Taylor-Restell, who used to run the great Restell wine auctions before Christie's took them over in 1966, told me that whenever such a story appeared he would get letters from people all over the country, some direct, some forwarded from Christie's or Sotheby's, asking him to sell such bottles. And he had to tell them that there is no such thing as a "Napoleon" brandy; that if there were, it would be undrinkable; and that the bottle, as likely as not, is one of those that Bisquit Dubouché used to offer before the war – and now, happily, no longer do – dated 1865, 1811, and even 1809. Many are still about, inherited from parents who are now piously imagined as having inherited them from theirs, whereas they had bought (for thirty shillings or so in those days) a brandy bearing a date only in the way that a sherry bears a solera date – not of a single, unblended vintage year, but of the earliest element in a blend, however minute.

It is not now permitted to do this; nor would any reputable firm such as Bisquit Dubouché do it. (Not that when they did so they intended to deceive, but the public now deceives itself.) For years now, such bottles, and even genuine older brandies, known to have been in bottle for a century and more, have been worth about eight or ten pounds at auction. This price remains pretty constant: Mr Taylor-Restell gave me this figure seven or eight years ago, and when Christie's held their first post-war wine sale in October 1966, after taking over Restells, and a very young television reporter sitting by me asked excitedly what I expected to be the top bid for the four bottles of Denis-Mounié Grande Champagne 1815, in authentically early bottles and from a well-known cellar, I told him – to his manifest disappointment – between eight and ten pounds and, sure enough, two went at ten pounds apiece, and two at seven pounds ten. Very properly, a bottle of Jameson's 1906 Irish whiskey fetched eleven pounds!

But however often facts such as these are made public, there are still people who think fondly of the fortune some dusty bottle is going to fetch them. I only wish it were true, and that I had had the commission on every bottle I have been asked to find a buyer for.

As for the name, "Napoleon", the word nowadays means simply that one particular firm, Courvoisier, advertises its cognac – I know not on what grounds – as, "the brandy of Napoleon"; and it has also become the custom of certain other firms to use the word "Napoleon" – or words or names carrying similar historical overtones, such as, "Aigle Impériale or (more modestly), "Louis Philippe" – to signify one of their finer blends, or the finest, certainly based on old brandies, but not necessarily dating from either Napoleon's time. In much the same way, in fact, as Moët et Chandon style their very finest champagne, "Dom Pérignon", without at all meaning to convey that what is in the bottle has been maturing since the days of that worthy seventeenth-century monk. (Only one cognac that I know of bears the name of an English monarch – the admirable Denis-Mounié "Edouard VII", a "tappit hen", or treble bottle, of which was presented to my son at his birth, and which I hope to do some damage to on his twenty-first birthday. But Edward VII lived just about the right number of years ago for the brandies of his time to be at their best.)

Among such brandies, are, for example, the Exshaw Fine Napoléon, of which the producers do not make any greater claim than that it is, "of extreme age"; and the Bisquit Dubouché Napoléon, which is a Grande Fine Champagne that the firm tells me, "contains brandies of between twenty and fifty years of age, and the resulting cognac has the keenness of young brandies combined with the bouquet of older cognacs". (It is amusing to note that the Bisquit Dubouché "Extra Vieille" is older than the Napoleon, and is a Grande Fine Champagne of an *average* age of forty-five to fifty years.)

These are two most reputable firms; their Napoleon brandies are of high quality; and, as will have been seen, they do not make extravagant claims as to their age. Nevertheless, I think it a pity that the name Napoleon should be used as loosely as it is, confusing the customer, even if unintentionally. I prefer the practice of, for instance, the house of Rémy-Martin, who produce only two qualities: a V.S.O.P. and a very distinguished cognac indeed, put up in a very swagger – and expensive – bottle, which they style simply, "Grande Champagne, Très Vieille, Age Inconnu" because, as their English shippers state in their publicity material, "although the blend from which it is made contains old cognacs taken from casks laid down an impressively long time ago, these casks have had to be refreshed from time to time and one cannot in honesty give any exact age to the brandy they now contain".

What is it, though, that I have by my elbow as I write? A bottle labelled, "Roullet and Delamain, Grande Champagne Cognac 1935"; and going on to say, "This Fine Old Cognac is from a cask matured in the London Docks since 1936 and was bottled in 1965 at the natural strength". I bought it from Corney and Barrow; it cost me only a few shillings more than a branded V.S.O.P.; I keep refilling my glass from it; it exemplifies the English taste I have already mentioned – for cognacs shipped here young and matured *in wood* under the damp English sky, losing strength but gaining softness, before being bottled. They are rare and expensive – it ties up a good deal of capital to keep casks of brandy here for so long. The French consider us mad to love them so much; they are certainly not for those who go to brandy for "kicks", but they have great charm for those who love old wines and who like to spend a reflective evening over a light and delicate liqueur. My own bottle here is little more than half the alcoholic strength of a commercial three-star V.S.O.P. – forty-five degrees proof compared with the usual seventy: "half-way between wine and brandy", said a fellow-director of the Directors' Wine Club as we tasted it before buying a couple of cases for our quarterly "Connoisseur's List", observing that he and I could finish the bottle between us, and come to no harm, and didn't I wish we had the time and the money.

Such brandies are referred to either as "early-landed" or "late-bottled", though Mr Edmund Penning-Rowsell of *The Financial Times*, who is – very properly – pedantic in these matters, maintains that a brandy can be "late-bottled" without being "early-landed", however long it has been in wood over here, if it was shipped into this country more than a year after the vintage: he would allow both descriptions to my Roullet and Delamain, vintage 1935, shipped 1936, bottled 1965.

Myself, I am inclined to be a little more lenient, especially as – since the French decree of 1962 – no brandy may come to this country with a certificate of age unless it is less than five years old, and this seems to me to be early-landed enough to warrant the honorific. Some old-established firms are still shipping some vintage brandies, with their age authenticated, to be matured here and sold eventually with both vintage and bottling dates on the label: even so extensive a chain of "popular" London off-licence shops as Stowells of Chelsea had, at the end of 1966, two early-landed Frapin brandies – a 1939 and a 1944, both bottled in December, 1959 – and, more heartening still, a 1945 and a 1950 still in cask, which it was intended to bottle in 1967 and 1968, respectively. And the private brandy-lover can always get his wine-merchant to import a hogshead of young brandy and keep it in wood for him, in a bonded cellar – at a couple of hundred pounds, a good investment, the duty not being paid until bottled and brought out of bond. Whenever I recall giving Mr Wynford Vaughan Thomas a glass of early-landed brandy, and his cry of "My God, Ray, this is what brandy is about!" I am tempted, myself, to do something of the sort.

Made in old-fashioned pot stills, and matured in oak, in pre-cisely the same way as cognac and as Highland malt whisky – not made in a patent still, like vodka and gin and the almost neutral grain whisky – is Irish whiskey, which spells itself with an "e", and with which, when in Ireland (and would that I were there more often) I invariably take my after-dinner coffee.

This in spite of the curious shyness of the waiters and bar-men in Irish hotels, both in Dublin and the countryside, about the noble wines of the country – whiskey and stout. Ask in an Irish hotel bar for whiskey, and one is offered Scotch; there is many a bar, and many an Aer Lingus aeroplane, where nobody knows how to make Black Velvet out of Guinness and champagne; some of the more swagger Dublin hotels, I am told, think it infra their dig to serve Guinness in the lounge; and although Irish wine-waiters are eager enough these days to offer you that very acceptable, but new-fangled and gimmicky confection, Irish coffee, of which more later, none has ever said to me, as I think he should, "I don't know what you thought of having with your coffee, sir, but we have a wonderful rare old Irish whiskey. . . ." What they offer is always "brandy or a liqueur, sir?" Yet at that splendid Dublin hotel, the Royal Hibernian (the restaurant of which I rank among the best half-dozen in the British Isles) I have succeeded in prising out of them a twenty-year-old John Jameson, bottled by Morgans of Dublin, which must have been a cut above even that ten-year-old Jameson that a member of the Hennessy family is said to have identified in Dublin as an 1893 Grande Champagne, and that on other occasions has been taken for an old *marc*.

I must confess that my own practice, in drinking Irish whiskey neat after dinner, is not that of the Irish themselves, who usually dilute it with rather less than the same amount of plain – never soda – water, and drink it at any hour of the day. "A ball o' malt" really is a phrase in current use in Ireland – not a stage Irishism, like "begorra" – and will buy you a glass of whiskey in any Irish pub. A large glass, indeed, for the kindly Irish serve a standard measure of two and a half ounces, whereas Scotland serves only two, and England a measly one and two-thirds. No wonder that Americans fall in love with Dublin's pubs, for in the United States a "shot" is a mere fluid ounce, and a "jigger" only one and a half.

But this means that the price of a ball o' malt drives the poor and the provident into asking for "a half one", which is still a sizeable tot, while not preventing some devotees of the creature from demanding a "tailor o' malt", which is a ball and a half, and recommended only to serious students. At the other end of the scale is the "whacker", which is no more than half of a half-one, and regarded as suitable only for impoverished old ladies.

Whereas the branded Scotch whiskies of commerce are blends of malt whisky from pot stills and grain whisky from patent stills, what blending there is of the well-known Irish brands is only of whiskeys that have all been made in the same way – three distillations in a pot still of a fermented mash of Irish barley, malted and unmalted, sometimes with wheat, oats and rye, though never I think with maize – but matured in different casks. At a tasting at Power's distillery in Dublin, for intance, I was shown no fewer than thirty-two different versions of the same whiskey – some from sherry casks, some from rum casks, some from American casks that had once held Bourbon and then been charred; some from storage in damp warehouses, some from dry; and of varying ages from seven to fifteen years – all destined to be blended into the standard Power's Gold Label. (No Irish whiskey is ever marketed before it is seven years old.)

They ranged in colour from that of the deepest brown sherry to the palest straw-yellow, according to what kind of cask they had been in, and for how long (the young spirit is colourless, and smells and tastes like such fruit *eaux-de-vie* as framboise or kirsch), and it was possible to detect in many of them the kind of cask they had come from – especially in those that had matured in rum barrels.

Some enthusiasts buy young whiskey and mature it themselves to a style of their own liking. Some buy single-cask whiskey rather than a blend: whiskey from old sherry casks is much sought after. But a firm such as Power's or Jameson's marries all the styles through a series of vattings, to produce its standard house style, and very good these branded Irish whiskeys are, and very honestly made. I have enjoyed the Gold Label, already mentioned, and Jameson's "Crested Ten", and at home I drink a Jameson twelve-year-old that is bottled and labelled for the Directors' Wine Club – the same whiskey, I think, that is sold as Jameson's "Redbreast": had the Irish distillers made the right sort of effort, at the right time, Irish whiskey might have won the cachet and the cash return in the United States – and through the demands of G.I.s and other globe-trotting Americans, in the rest of the world – now enjoyed by Scotch. It is more specifically and uniquely Irish than the standard Scotch blends can claim, in spite of their evocative names and trade-marks and *New Yorker* advertisements, to be uniquely Scotch, for the patent-still grain whisky that is blended with the malt whisky from the pot stills to make the Scotch whisky of commerce is made of maize from the United States itself, from South Africa or, more and more these days, from the other side of the iron curtain. The last time I visited a distillery in Scotland I arrived at the same time as a load of maize in bags boldly labelled "Rumania".

Of course, the Irish distilleries do not have anything approaching the capacity to satisfy the demand there is now for Scotch, but there could have been expansion, and I should have liked to see them sharing, at any rate, the prosperity and the prestige that whisky has earned for Scotland.

The Irish licensing laws are more lunatic even than those of the neighbouring island. Many restaurants have only a wine licence, which means that they cannot serve Guinness with

oysters, or a gin before dinner or even Irish whiskey afterwards. But by a benign quirk Irish coffee is legally a "cooked
dish", exempt from the restriction and, being a beverage
that not only cheers but, taken in sufficient quantities, ineb-
riates, has reconciled many a tourist to having been deprived
of his pre-prandial martini.

This is the way it is made. In a heated glass (tall, and preferably with a stem, for this is a hot drink) put a measure of
Irish whiskey and sugar, both in amounts to the taste that you
will develop in the course of experiment. I think that the
Irish themselves give it a full measure of whiskey – two and a
half ounces. Fill with strong, hot, black coffee to within about
an inch of the brim. Stir thoroughly. Then pour double
cream on to the surface, very gently, so that it does not
mix – pouring it over the back of a spoon, as the Viennese
do, is the best method. The object is to drink the strong,
sweet, hot, black-coffee-and-whiskey-and-sugar through,
with, and in contrast to the cold, bland, blond cream. This
is why it is essential that the stirring be done *before* the cream
is added.

Not being an Irishman, I cannot believe that the curse of
Cromwell will fall upon you if you use Scotch whisky and
call it Highland coffee, or if you use brandy, in which case, I
am told, its name is Gaelic coffee, though what the Gaels have
to do with brandy I do not know – unless it consoles them for
being Gaels. Or unless it was originally not "Gaelic", but
"Gallic".

But the comforting concoction in its classic manifestation
has become so widely known, and has done so much for the
Irish distilleries that a couple of years ago the Irish Government's Department of External Affairs actually devoted a
page of its fortnightly *Bulletin* to discussing the question of its
origin, which is as though the Foreign Office had issued a

scholarly statement about mild and bitter, or the State
Department spoken authoritatively on martinis.

According to this pronouncement – based on researches
conducted by a Captain P. D. O'Donnell for an Irish newspaper – it was Joe Sheridan, the then chef at Shannon Airport's restaurant who, in the late nineteen-thirties, hit upon
the idea of serving a group of belated Americans, cold and
tired, with hot coffee laced with whiskey and topped with
cream.

Even then, the *Bulletin* admits, the idea may not have been
entirely original,* but it was enthusiastically written about by
a journalist from the *San Francisco Chronicle*, which caused it
to be taken up as a speciality of the house by a San Francisco
restaurant, whence the cult spread along the western seaboard
of the United States before crossing to New York. And it was
by way of New York that the fashion for this Irish cockle-
warmer came back to Europe from California.

And I hope to see some time the Foreign Office writing as
rhapsodically about anything as the Irish Department of
External Affairs writes about, "the creative spirit of Joe
Sheridan, whose deep compassion for his fellow human beings,
his artist's eye and gourmet's palate fused on that cold wintry
night in the late 'thirties by 'the dark mutinous waves of the
Shannon' to dream up the delight that is Irish coffee".

It was on another Irish wintry day that I encountered an
acceptable variant of Mr Sheridan's *chef d'œuvre*. I had persuaded the editor of an English magazine that I should crack

---

* My copy of Eliza Acton's *Modern Cookery*, which is the 1863 edition, has a
recipe for "BURNT COFFEE, OR COFFEE A LA MILITAIRE (*in France vulgarly called
Gloria*): Make some coffee as strong and clear as possible, sweeten it in the cup
with white sugar almost to syrup, then pour the brandy on the top gently over
a spoon, set fire to it with a lighted paper" (taper?) "and when the spirit is in
part consumed, blow out the flame, and drink the *gloria* quite hot."

a bottle of that other admirable Irish whiskey, Tullamore
Dew, at Tullamore, and I was duly collected in Dublin by my
claret-drinking crony, Tom Whelehan, who is half my age
and has drunk twice as much wine, to be taken by train across
the Bog of Allen to the town of Tullamore – the town that
has given its name to one of the most notable of Irish whiskeys.
(But that Berlin barman is going to be disappointed who,
created a freeman of Tullamore for his services to the Irish
whiskey trade, fondly hopes that when he sets foot in Tullamore for the first time it is going to be one long round of chic
restaurants and cheeky night clubs.)

Everyone in Ireland knows everyone else. "Give my love
to Desmond Williams", Bryan Guinness had said, "and
especially to Brenda – she's the daughter of Oliver Gogarty,
don't you know, and she sculpted my children."

And so I conveyed greetings from the Dublin brewer to
the Tullamore distiller while he made hospitable noises with
bottles of his Dew, which we drank as an eye-opener before
luncheon, with rather less than the same amount of water,
and I sat at the window, my attention divided between my
host and hostess and their paintings, and the view across the
soft, green plain to the slow, smooth, flattened curves of
Slieve Bloom, speckled with snow and blurred a little with
winter mist. "Call zem mountains!" a German *au pair* girl
once said to Brenda Williams: "I could *shpit* across zem!"

But the placid enjoyment with which I was drinking my
whiskey was shattered when Desmond Williams broke it to
me that while it was true that there I was, cracking a bottle of
Tullamore Dew at Tullamore, he would be very much
obliged if I would write about something else for my
admirable magazine – the fact being that they had sold the
name to their old friends and rivals, Powers of Dublin, who
would now be making Tullamore Dew in the very city I had

left that morning to come to taste the whiskey that he would not be making there any more.

And if it is difficult to avoid the observation that there is something very Irish in inviting a man half way across your country to tell him that he need not have come, it is only fair to add that it is equally Irish to seize upon any excuse to bring one who is a complete stranger, but known to be a friend of friends, half way round the world, if necessary, to stretch his legs beneath your mahogany, and drink your claret.

For there is a great claret-drinking tradition in Ireland, still, and just as I had drunk Vieux Château Certan 1947 with Bryan Guinness, the brewer, at Knockmaroon the night before, so now, with an Irish distiller, I drank Mouton-Roths-child 1953, which struck me as very handsome amends, and then a fine old cognac that I had not met before, but should not mind meeting again, until the coffee came and, with it, the liqueur that the Tullamore people still make, and that must go a long way towards reconciling them to the thought that the Dew itself is now distilled in Dublin.

Irish Mist is to Irish whiskey what Drambuie is to Scotch – with heather-honey and herbs to thicken and sweeten and flavour the basic spirit, which in this case is fifteen-year-old Irish whiskey. But I have always preferred the Irish liqueur, which is darker in colour, and smokier and fuller in flavour to the Scotch. We drank it neat, which is a bit sweet for me, and we drank it half-and-half with Tullamore Dew, in the way that one drinks brandy with Benedictine, to preserve the flavour while diminishing the sweetness, and then Brenda Williams made Irish Mist coffee* for us, which is not quite

* There is one other Irish liqueur – Irish Coffee Liqueur, not to be confused with Irish coffee itself, but a sweet after-dinner drink made at Waterford of Irish whiskey, honey, herbs and coffee essence, in style not unlike Tia Maria. This, too, gains in my opinion by being mixed half-and-half with any Irish whiskey.

the same thing as Irish coffee, but a similar bit of all right.

It is made in precisely the same way as Irish coffee, save that with Irish Mist instead of Irish whiskey there is no need for sugar, and there is an additional subtle taste of herbs. We tried one part of Irish Mist to four of coffee, decided that there was not enough Irish Mist, and went back to Irish Mist and Tullamore Dew, just to keep us occupied, while our hostess concocted for us another brew of one liqueur to three of coffee.

This, we decided, was it – not too sweet and not too dry, and insidiously bland, so that a man might be enveloped in a gentle and consoling haze before he had even noticed that the sun had gone in.

And thus it was that I left Tullamore that afternoon, enveloped in a sort of Irish mist of my own, engendered by the Irish Mist within – not to mention the pre-prandial whiskey, the brandy I had not met before but should not mind meeting again, and the Château Mouton-Rothschild 1953 – back to the city where they distil Tullamore Dew, the city I had left that morning for Tullamore.

I think as highly of the single-malt (or "straight malt", or "Highland malt"), which is to say unblended, Highland whiskies as I do of the Irish, and wish only that I knew as much about them, but there are many more, and they differ more widely in style and character between themselves. All the Scotch whiskies of commerce are blends of these Highland malts with grain whiskies. To put it only very roughly and very generally, the average branded blend is likely to be about 60 per cent patent-still whisky made of unmalted grain (usually maize from the United States, South Africa or Central Europe) and 40 per cent pot-still whisky made of malted Scottish barley.

The grain whisky gives lightness, the malt whisky flavour: so much so, indeed, that some Dutch distillers are importing malt whisky from Scotland to mix with locally-distilled neutral spirits and thus make a very passable Dutch "Scotch". (The well-known firms, especially those in the Distillers' Company, are cagey about the proportions in their blends, and will not even discuss differences in style between one brand and another, as the relaxed and civilized champagne families will about their wines.) But there are those – many unsophisticated Highlanders, such as ghillies and shepherds, and a few sophisticated Londoners and New Yorkers and the like – who have an especial interest in and affection for a straight, unblended malt whisky, and who roll the names of Laphroaig and Craigellachie and Glenmorangie as lovingly around their tongues as they do the noble tipples themselves.

There are wide differences between the products of the various pot-still distilleries. I have a long-standing open invitation to a comparative tasting at Fortnum and Mason's wine department, which has what is probably the longest list of single malts held by any retail shop – a score or so, from Glenfiddich to Glen Grant, by way of Glenfarchas and Glen Mhor, to say nothing of Glen Moray and Glenmorangie, all the way to the fifteen-year-old Strathisla, at a 100 degrees proof (standard blends are seventy). It would be wrong to assume that these majestic nectars are necessarily heavier on the head or the digestion than the blends (many, in spite of that Strathisla, are no stronger alcoholically, or only a little so, and their apparent greater "heaviness" is a matter of flavour and texture, not of alcohol). But such is the potency of their very names that I have always felt that I should need a fortnight away from my desk to do justice to so awe-inspiring an experiment: a week of prayer and fasting beforehand, and a week at Baden-Baden or Enton Hall afterwards.

So I rely as much on the researches of others as on my own for the information that the single malts from Campbeltown and Islay are characteristically smoky in flavour, the Campbeltowns being used only for blending, while Islay produces the famous Islay Mist and Laphroaig; that Glenmorangie and Dalmore have more malt and less peat in their taste; those from Skye – such as Talisker – being fuller and peatier. From Speyside comes, among other aristocrats of the race, the fabled Glenlivet, celebrated in song and story, which Walter Scott hailed as the greatest of them all.

I remember sitting one day over fine boiled Scotch salmon in the dining-room of the Turnberry Hotel with Sandy Grant Gordon, great-grandson of the William Grant who founded Grant's Glenfiddich distillery. The sun flicked glints of gold from the waters of the Firth of Clyde: between Arran and the Mull of Kintyre, blue and pale violet in the distance, rose the dark lump of Ailsa Craig, out of which they quarry the curling-stones, and between Sandy and me stood a bottle of Grant's Glenfiddich, the straight malt whisky that is still made at the same place on Speyside, "distilled and matured", states the label, "according to the methods of the first William Grant of Glenfiddich", and brought down to strength with the same local spring water that goes to its making.

We drank it before our luncheon as an aperitif with about half the same amount of water, my host maintaining that this releases the fragrance and the flavour, though he expressed disapproval of iced water, as numbing those very qualities, and the gravest doubts about London's heavily chlorinated water: in London, he said, he took a bottled table water with it – either the completely neutral Malvern water, or Perrier. But I enjoyed it better neat after luncheon, with coffee, when I became more aware of the top soft sweetness, deriving from the sherry casks in which it had matured, and then the drier, smoky under-flavour. It seemed to me drier than the heavily aromatic Laphroaig and Mackenzie's splendid twenty-year-old Dalmore, the other malts I know best, and not quite so bland, either in mouth or in belly, as the best Irish, but still with the characteristic peaty, smoky flavour of a single malt, and the "weight" that is deliberately diminished in the well-known blends by the addition of grain whisky, or the lighter Lowland malts.

I learned over my Glenfiddich how, as with Irish, whiskies are blended that have all been distilled in the same way, but matured in different casks, and for varying lengths of time. The youngest whisky in this particular mixture is eight years old, most are ten or eleven, and there are some as old as fourteen or so. Glenfiddich is not caramelled to a standard colour, as the blended whiskies must be, however slightly, and as are far too many even of the very best brandies – I doubt whether any of the great Highland malts is. The very pale straw colour, which may vary from bottle to bottle, according to the batch it has come from, derives solely from the wood. Indeed, paleness is a virtue in malt whisky, and some distillers have tried to make their fine malts completely colourless by filtering through charcoal, but this, instead of softening them, as one might expect, seems to restore a youthful fieriness.

What else I learned about Glenfiddich was that the countryside in which it stands, in Strath Spey, is so remote yet and untouched that the golden eagle still nests there, and in the trees – not, as elsewhere, among the rocks – and that the William Grant who built the distillery at Glenfiddich in 1887 did so with his own hands and those of his sons and daughters, carefully noting in his final accounts, as a self-help Victorian Scotsman should, "To paper for plans of distillery, one shilling".

I have never been able to understand why we do not make dry brandies in this country out of the fruits we grow so easily and so well. It seems to me that we are as wasteful with our splendid crops of apples, cherries and plums, out of which more provident peasantries abroad distil such potent delicacies as calvados, kirsch, mirabelle and slivovitz, as our hill-farmers are in not making a sheep's-milk cheese, and thus obliging us to eat expensively imported Roquefort, or to put up with that salty simulacrum that the Danes sell us so much of.

(Ask a sheep-farmer why he doesn't make a sheep's-milk cheese, and his answer is that the British public wouldn't eat it – they are too conservative, he says. Point out that the most widely sold blue cheese in Britain is a Danish imitation of a French sheep's-milk cheese, and he shrugs his shoulders. I have never dared yet to point out that it is the farmer that is conservative, not the public. The British public, as every advertising man knows, is so far from being conservative in it eating habits that it will eat anything.)

I am not referring here to the sweet liqueurs, which are cordials rather than brandies, though I respect the sloe gin made by Hawkers of Plymouth, and Grant's Morella Cherry Brandy. The best after-dinner drink I have met of this kind, though, is one that my wife and I make at home, by dividing equally among enough kilner jars to take it, a mixture of three bottles of London gin, four pounds of sound ripe damsons, wiped but not washed, and cut deeply round their middles, and a pound of caster sugar. We screw up the jar tightly, shake every day for at least three months, after which the liqueur is strained off and bottled – dry, but fruity, not at all cloying, as are some of the patent after-dinner drinks, with a most beautiful colour and a marked plummy taste. A

admirable after-dinner liqueur and, like the traditional sloe
gin and cherry brandy, just the thing for the flask on a hunting
morning. No reason, for that matter, why anti-blood-
sporters should not also take it out on false-trail-layings, and
jolly good luck to them, say I.

But what I had in mind were the dry colourless *eaux de vie*
that the French call *alcools blancs*, distilled from fermented
fruit, such as Germans and Alsatians and Yugoslavs drink,
cold and neat, as *schnapps*, before and between meals, but which
I like – when I can afford them, for in this country they are
very dear – as austere after-dinner liqueurs. Once upon a time,
it seems, they used to make an applejack in the West country
from English apples (which is more than can be said of some
of our English ciders, these days), for Maurice Healy recorded
that he once drank an eighty-year-old English applejack and
a French calvados of the same age, and found nothing to
choose between them – they both gave him indigestion. In
Alsace, on the other hand, there are said to be seventeen
different kinds of fruit brandy, though even when in Alsace
itself I have been unable to identify all of them precisely.
Kirsch and framboise are easy and it is possible, reminded of
poire William, quetsch and mirabelle, along with a couple of
others, to tot up eight or nine. But when I set a director of the
Dolfi distillery in Strasbourg to tell me what others he knew
of – some of them produced only in tiny quantities by small
farmers in the Vosges – we managed to name seventeen between us only by his including some that I could not relate to
any fruit that I knew the name of in English. Neither draw-
ings nor a dictionary helped me to discover what *alizier* is, for
instance: the dictionary called it a beam-tree, whatever that
may be. *Sorbes* was defined as being a sorb-apple: I am only
half sure that it is a rowan, and not all that more definite in
identifying *sureau* as the elderberry.

My own contribution was *baie de houx*, which to my delight even the distiller had never heard of – an *eau de vie* distilled from holly berries which, at my hotel in the Vosges, cost twice as much even as framboise, and was not half so nice. My expert friend told me that it must have been the produce of one of the neighbouring mountain farmers, some of whom distil *eau de vie* from anything they can lay their hands on, whether out of enthusiasm in a hobby, or out of French peasant canniness, or in the spirit of that French gourmet who said that the good Lord had intended all living things for man to eat, and that only owls and black beetles had shaken him in his faith.

The commercial distilleries complain that some of the farmers who still have a licence to distil for their own consumption (a class that is dying out, as new licences are not being issued) spoil the home trade by encouraging a sort of black market among local consumers. Those farmers who do not distil for themselves, but sell their fruit to the distilleries, complain that they cannot get pickers, and that a good deal of wild fruit, especially, such as bilberries, blackberries and wild raspberries, for myrtille, mure and framboise, now remains ungathered.

It looks as though kirsch and poire William (and calvados, from Normandy), being from cultivated fruits, easier to pick, will increase their pre-eminence in the market, though I see that the London house of George Idle, Chapman, swimming against the tide, are now shipping quetsch, mirabelle and framboise as well from the Cusenier distillery at Mulhouse. My own preference is for the framboise and the poire William, but I think that this is because I drink them rarely, and that if I drank them more often I would turn to one of the plum liqueurs for a change, as having a less emphatic flavour. All the Cusenier *eaux de vie* are dry and delicate – too many of

the commercial brands that I have come across lately seem to
have had their flavours artificially enhanced, and to have been
artificially sweetened.

At tastings both of the Dolfi and the Cusenier *eaux de vie*,
I have found it difficult to distinguish between the quetsch,
which is made from a small, purple plum, and the mirabelle,
from a golden, and I think, a sweeter plum, though I understand that the mirabelle is more highly regarded by connois-
seurs. With all of them, it is important that they should be
drunk ice-cold, from glasses that have previously been chilled
– this brings out the flavour of the fruit.

The Alsatians take great pride in these strong colourless
brandies, as well they might, and it irks them to have to
apply the word "brandy" to the more lusciously sweet and
alcoholically weaker liqueurs, such as apricot brandy, peach
brandy, and cherry brandy, because of confusion in the public
mind between two quite different things – one that really *is* a
brandy, in being distilled from fermented fruits, as cognac is
from wine, and the others being really sweetened cordials,
many of them good of their kind (I am very fond of the
apricot brandy made by Henkes of Rotterdam), but pretty
little liquid sweetmeats compared with the potent hard stuff
of Alsace.

And even the biggest and most prosperous of the Alsatian
distilleries are jealous of the solid success of the cognac houses.
"They make quite a good *eau de vie*, I suppose," one Stras-
bourgeois said to me, in that splendidly grudging tone that
all Frenchmen use of the products of any region other than
their own, "but after all, it's only made out of bad wine, such
as you wouldn't dream of drinking. Look at the good fruit
we use!"

9 · Cups, Mulls, Punches & Grogs

Claret cup is like fish-cakes, or shepherd's pie. It is to be regarded with caution by the discriminating guest: if the host is mean, or merely lacking in taste, it will be a cheap and nasty way of using left-overs, or of making a little in the larder go a long way in the dining-room. But if the host is a man of taste, it can be delicious – just as the very best shepherd's pie is, or fish-cakes made, as fish-cakes should be, of salmon.

Wine cups should invigorate as well as refresh: were it only a matter of quenching our summertime thirsts, we should drink ice-cold fresh orange-juice, or peach tea, or home-made lemonade, and very good these are, too. But the idea of a wine cup is that it should provide enough alcohol to stimulate those jaded by the summer heat, to encourage conversation and appetite, or to induce a garden-party spirit. So, although it must look refreshing, and be diluted enough to be drunk in thirst-quenching quantities without going to the head under a hot sun, it must not be so weakened with soda water, melting ice, and disintegrating tinned fruit as to be depressing. It should also taste of something, so my firm belief is that one should use as little ice as will cool the cup or, better still, do without it altogether by keeping the mixed drink in a refrigerator or an ice-bucket, or in one of those jugs or carafes with a separate ice-container.

I have written approvingly, in another chapter, about Black Velvet and about Buck's Fizz, but there are those – myself not among them – who find merit in the so-called champagne cocktail, a time-honoured recipe for which adds a glass of brandy and two slices of orange, a twist apiece of lemon peel and cucumber, and a sprig of borage or verbena to a bottle of champagne. Leave for half an hour in a cold refrigerator, or else add ice, and serve. This seems to me a waste of borage.

Champagne figures, too, in one of the drier versions of claret cup, made with equal quantities of claret and champagne, with one glass of any orange liqueur to every two bottles of the mixture, the zest of a lemon, and sugar. But Badminton cup is fruitier: pour a bottle of claret over half a cucumber, peeled and sliced, the juice of a lemon, a pinch of nutmeg, half a glass of any orange liqueur and sugar. When the sugar is dissolved, pour in a bottle of soda water, add ice if necessary, and garnish with borage or cucumber peel.

Among red-wine cups there must be a place for the Spanish sangria, a simple version of which calls for a bottle of red wine (Spanish if possible, of course, such as a red Rioja); about a quarter as much soda water; a heaped egg-cup of sugar already dissolved in water; half a lemon and a couple of oranges, sliced; and some or all of the following – a pear, a banana, a fresh peach and a slice of melon – all diced and mixed; the whole served very cold, after a substantial pinch of cinnamon has been stirred in at the last minute. Cubes of ice may be added, and so may a sherry-glass of brandy to every bottle.

I am not all that fond, myself, of heaps of fruit swimming about in watered-down wine – melon mixes well enough, but apples and pears and bananas soon look very tired – yet I have happy memories of sangria parties under English skies, and travellers tell me that in Spain itself, a country I do not know, *sangria seca*, which omits the sugar, is notably refreshing. It is drunk a good deal in southern Spain, particularly, and I wonder whether they put sherry in the mixture there, or stick to Spanish brandy as a strengthener.

Experts on things Spanish assure me that the pinch of cinnamon is of the utmost importance, and that sangria is not sangria without it. Which reminds me that in the United States chilled and sweetened mixtures of wines, beers or spirits are known as sangarees – which, I take it, derive their characters and their names from sangria – and are always dusted over the top with grated nutmeg. When I looked up an American book on mixed drinks to confirm this recollection, I discovered that even a recipe for a sangaree made of beer or stout – a long glass of either, chilled, sweetened with two teaspoons of sugar melted in water, and stirred – still required the ritual dusting of grated nutmeg.

I have not tried stout and nutmeg: it is curious how little we experiment with our own wines of the country – beer, stout and cider – in making mixed drinks, cups and mulls, compared with our enterprise and ingenuity in dressing up the more exotic mixtures from abroad. Still, I have heard of a cider cup made by adding a wine-glass apiece of sherry and of brandy to a quart flagon of sweet cider, with a bottle of soda water,

ᵣe juice of half a lemon with its zest, sugar, nutmeg and some
ᵤcumber rind. Or a pint of cider, a pint of ginger ale, and a
ᵣnall glass of brandy make Bull's Eye, which is quite the best
ᵣing to do with the commercial ciders of our time, which
ᵣem to me to owe more to the advertising copywriter than
ᵣ tradition.*

The best of beer cups is shandy, which is short for shandy-
aff, a name now never heard, which consists of equal quanti-
ᵣs of beer and ginger-beer (*not* fizzy lemonade), served very
ᵣld; though some may like to experiment with an ale punch
ᵣade by adding a wine-glass each of sherry and of brandy to
ᵣ quart bottle of brown ale, with the peel and the juice of one
ᵣmon, a tablespoon of sugar, a pinch of nutmeg (as in an
ᵣmerican sangaree) and a little ice.

Leaving beer for more exotic beverages, a particularly frag-
ᵣnt cup is made by adding a quarter of a bottle of an orange
ᵣqueur to one of dry vermouth, with a dash of orange bitters
ᵣd two bottles of soda water. But there are many variants of
ᵣe vermouth theme: a millionaire member of the Directors'
ᵣVine Club invented a delicious long cool drink that consisted
ᵣf 50 per cent vin rosé, 35 per cent soda water, and 15 per
ᵣnt Nivolet, the Club's wild-strawberry-flavoured Cham-
ᵣéry vermouth, which is the same thing as the Chambéryzette
ᵣlready mentioned in my chapter on short drinks.

That admirable firm, Pimm's, has made things easy for
ᵣose who like long spirit-based slings rather than wine cups.
ᵣSling", according to M André Simon's *Concise Encylo-
ᵣaedia of Gastronomy*, "is the name given to a number of cold
ᵣnixed beverages, more particularly popular in the tropics",
ᵣnd goes on to give only one recipe, culled from an American
ᵣork, which calls not only for lime-juice, cherry brandy, gin,
ᵣe, seltzer, orange and mint, but also for Bénédictine and

* See, though, the footnote on p. 117.

brandy to be added by the drop, "through the middle with
medicine dropper". The beauty of the various Pimm's prep
rations, even for those who, like me, prefer to know what
in their drinks and their food, and the Pimm's labels a
pretty uncommunicative, is that they minimize the numb
of various ingredients, besides dispensing altogether with tl
need for a medicine dropper, an implement that seldom seen
to be at hand when needed.

One should not confine oneself to Pimm's Number 1, tl
gin sling, good as it is (it seems to be the only one that barme
know, or their employers stock), nor should it be served, d
accepted, with one of those beastly, bright red "cocktai.
cherries in it, which do not give the sling a chance to taste d
anything else. A slice of lemon and a twist of cucumber rin
is all that the admirable drink requires, unless there is boraz
available, in which case it takes the place of the cucumbe
which it is said to resemble in taste and in cooling propertie
and which I have heard of but never seen. And the recon
mended proportions should be adhered to – too much mi:
ture to too little lemonade and ice makes it too sweet. Tl
ideal helping is about as long and as strong as a gin-and-ton
or a fairly conventional whisky-and-soda.

The Number 2 is made of Scotch and seems to me to hav
more character than the Number 1 or the Number 3, base
on brandy, which I have found disappointing – I am told
should try it with ginger ale instead of the usual fizzy lemor
ade. Number 4, the rum sling, is my favourite, and ovei
shadows – to my taste – both the Number 5, made of ry
whisky, and the Number 6, of vodka, which is not, in m
opinion, a drink for this kind of treatment.

For those who like to make their own slings, and are pre
pared to do without the *Concise Encyclopaedia*'s medicir
dropper and battery of ingredients, the famous Singapore gi

sling is basically a mixture of two parts of cherry brandy to one of gin, with lemon juice (or fresh lime juice), a dash of Angostura bitters, soda water and ice, served in tumblers. And a heartening Brandy Fix consists of one teaspoon of sugar dissolved in one of water, the juice of half a lemon, two liqueur glasses of brandy and one of cherry brandy, all in a tumbler filled with crushed ice, with a slice of lemon added, and drunk through a straw.

The various light, dry, white rums lend themselves admirably to making long, cooling drinks – indeed, such a rum can be substituted for brandy in the previous recipe. And white rum and tonic water, with a cube of ice and a slice of lemon is as notable a cooler as the better-known gin and tonic. But the celebrated Planter's Punch is usually made of the more aromatic Jamaica rum – two of rum to one of lime juice, a dessertspoon of sugar dissolved in water, a dash of Angostura, with a slice of pineapple and one of orange, also drunk through a straw.

In this country, we think of whisky as a warmer, but it is the basis of one of the most famous of all long, cooling drinks, the Kentucky mint julep. But this should be made with American bourbon, and to be done properly requires a skilled barman's expert attentions. Anyone, though, can make a whisky punch on the same principle as a Planter's Punch – equally admirable whether made with Scotch or Irish, bourbon or rye. It follows the old formula of, "one of sweet, two of sour, three of strong and four of weak" – one part, that is, of sugar dissolved in water or (better still) of an orange-flavoured liqueur; two of lemon juice; three of whisky; and four of soda water. I am told that there are Americans who reverse the proportions of strong and weak. The first three ingredients are shaken with some crushed ice, and the fourth is used to top up the glasses: a dash of Angostura does no harm. Decorate with fruit or mint or both, and serve with straws for drinking through.

Of white-wine mixtures, there is much to be said for *vin blanc cassis*, which is a glass of cold, dry or dryish white wine, with a teaspoon or so in it of *crème de cassis*, the sweet, fortified blackcurrant cordial. The classic place for *crème de cassis* is Dijon, and in France this mixture is sometimes called *un Kyr*, after the Canon Kyr, who was a stubbornly patriotic mayor of the city during the German occupation, and sturdily left-wing after it. *Crème de cassis* goes well, too, with dry vermouth, ice and soda water, as *vermouth cassis*, and a substitution of our own Ribena concentrated blackcurrant juice for the French cordial need not be despised, for the *cassis* is high in sugar and low in alcohol, and little kick is lost in the exchange.

In the Rhineland, the wine-growers go in for a mixed summertime drink called *kalte Ente* ("cold duck" – do not ask me why). They mix two bottles of still hock or Mosel with one of sparkling, add a small bottle of soda water, and the zest of a lemon. Ice, I think, is never added: the drink is always served in a glass jug with a separate ice-container. Such jugs are to be found everywhere in the Rhineland, sometimes very elaborately cut, and silver-mounted. Dr Fritz Hallgarten, in his book *Rhineland-Wineland*, omits the soda water, says that the proportion of sparkling wine may be increased, and recommends slices of lemon, to be removed after a short time, a glass of orange liqueur, and sugar to taste.

But then there is nothing sacred about this or any other recipe for cups – proportions can be varied to taste (which gives ample excuse for experiment). After all, even Professor Saintsbury, pedantic in so much else, when giving a recipe for his own cup – one bottle of claret to half a bottle of Mosel, thick slices of pineapple, and "one lump of ice as big as a baby's head" – did not trouble to give the age of the baby.

I claim for my own summer wine cup a noble simplicity, for it consists of nothing more than one bottle of claret to one of champagne, one glass of brandy, and one of Grand Marnier, with the zest of a lemon and caster sugar to taste, completely undiluted, and served very cold without the addition of ice. This is expensive, reassuring, and refreshing, less for garden parties than for a warm evening after a trying day, and is not for young things unless you have designs on them.

Mulled wine goes well with mists, mellow fruitfulness and the general miseries of an English autumn. What is more, it is easy to make. There is only one basic rule, which is that wine should be heated gently, never boiled; and the necessary equipment is small – a saucepan, glass mugs with handles (mulled wine should be served too hot to hold in a thin wine-glass), a spoon to each glass to prevent its cracking, and a big jug or bowl standing on some sort of hot-plate, whether electric or heated by night-light candles.

The classic French *vin chaud* consists merely of a bottle of red wine warmed up with half as much water, a sherry glass of brandy, a couple of lumps of sugar, a pinch or so of cinnamon or nutmeg, and a slice of lemon to each glass.

The Austrian *gluehwein* is much the same, save that the Austrians use a lighter wine (they are great drinkers of the light wines of the Italian Lakes, such as Valpolicella), omit the water, and like to add cloves. But there is a much more lordly drink from these parts, which the Viennese call *Lebensretter*, or Life-saver, and with some justification, for it is nothing more nor less than a bottle of port to half a bottle of brandy, mixed, sugared to taste, and served very hot. Not for babies.

Everybody expects a mulled wine to be red in colour, and

deep red at that, but there is at any rate one white-wine mull, the recipe for which was given a few winters ago in Harvey's wine list. They called it Harveys' Specifick, and recommended it as, "an efficacious remedy against rheums and the ague", which strikes me as probable enough, for it adds a glass of brandy to half a bottle of dry white wine, the juice of half a lemon and three dessertspoons of honey, before heating the mixture.

Nor is wine the only liquor meet to be mulled: beer, too, can warm the cockles on a winter's evening. I owe to a book entitled *Cooling Cups and Dainty Drinks* this recipe for a drink that is neither cooling nor particularly dainty – the celebrated Lamb's Wool, or Brasenose Ale, already time-honoured when my source-book was published, in 1869: Pepys had written two centuries earlier of, "cards till two in the morning, drinking Lamb's Wool".

The way to make it is to bake eight apples in the oven, mash them and add a quart of old ale; put the lot through a sieve; add ground ginger, nutmeg and sugar, all to taste; warm and drink while warm.

Draught mild brought from the pub in a jug, or brown ale in flagons, will do very well for this drink. The apple mush gives a fleecy froth to the mulled beer – hence the name. Another version adds a pint of white wine to the quart of beer – Yugoslav riesling will do.

Auld Man's Milk is stronger: it adds to a pint of warmed Scotch ale – and again, draught mild or bottled brown will do – a quarter-ounce each of powdered cinnamon, powdered ginger and grated nutmeg, the yolks of two eggs with a little brown sugar, and a glass of whisky. Add the spices to the ale while it is warming; the mixture is then poured slowly on to the beaten-up eggs and sugar, and the whisky is added at the last, when all is well blended.

Much simpler is spiced ale. For this you can use any
ordinary beer (I think that for all mulling purposes the milder,
sweeter beers are more suitable than the drier, more heavily
hopped ones). Bring it almost, but not quite, to boiling, with
a pinch or so of nutmeg, a twist of lemon peel, brown sugar
to taste and, at the last moment, a sherry glass of brandy.

Similarly comforting on a cold night is a hot grog made of
rum: usually this is made by the glass, by pouring a tot of
dark rum, such as Jamaica, into a half-pint glass mug, adding a
tablespoon of lemon juice, about a teaspoon of sugar, and
filling up with hot Indian tea, not too strong. Garnish with a
twist of lemon peel. Use hot water instead of tea, put in three
or four whole cloves, float a walnut-sized piece of butter on
top, stirring it gently until it dissolves, and you have hot
buttered rum, which is much admired and enjoyed by some,
though I incline myself to the view of the American authority
who insisted that indulgence in hot buttered rum should be
confined to the Northwest Passage, and then only in novels
written by women.

Strictly speaking, punches are cold, not hot, though there
are exceptions. One of the most famous cold punches is
Philadelphia Fish-House Punch, named after an eighteenth-
century Philadelphia club or tavern, which I always think we
should make a family speciality of, for my wife has a female
ancestor born to an officer serving in the American colonies
before the rebellion, whose name was Philadelphia Penfound.

There are many recipes, one of the best of which calls for a
quarter of a pint of peach brandy, half a pint of cognac, a
quarter of a pint of Jamaica rum, a third of a pint of lemon
juice, three-quarters of a pound of white sugar, and two and a
half pints of cold water. What has always impressed me is
that in *How to Mix Drinks, or the Bon Vivant's Companion*,
published in New York in 1862, which I have already quoted

in my chapter on short drinks, the author, Jerry Thoma
opined that this quantity of the mixture, "is generally su
ficient for one person". I do not doubt it.

One of the exceptions to the rule that punches are co
mixtures is the brandy-and-rum recipe given by Jerry Thoma
"For a party of fifteen," it runs, "take one quart of Jamaic
rum, one quart of Cognac brandy, one pound of white loa
sugar, four lemons, three quarts of boiling water and on
teaspoon of nutmeg. Rub the sugar over the lemons until
has absorbed all the yellow part of the skins, then put th
sugar into a punch-bowl and pour over it the boiling wate
stir well together; add the rum, brandy and nutmeg; mi
thoroughly, and the punch will be ready to serve."

In the same redoubtable work is a recipe for the drin
called Rocky Mountain Punch, subtitled, "For a Mixe
Party of Twenty: From a Recipe in the Possession of Majc
James Foster". It is compounded of five bottles of champagn
a quart of Jamaica rum, a pint of maraschino, six slice
lemons and sugar to taste, all mixed in a large punch-bow
with a large square block of ice in the middle, ornamente
with fruit. Jerry Thomas adds that, "this is a splendid punc
for New Year's Day". Why, I do not know, unless it serve
to restore a Mixed Party of Twenty (including Major Jame
Foster) after whatever it was that they had been up to on Ne
Year's Eve. In the Rocky Mountains.

10 · *In Partibus Infidelium*

When James Thurber penned under his *New Yorker* cartoon that all-too-frequently quoted caption, "It's a naïve domestic burgundy without any breeding, but I think you will be amused by its presumption", it was specifically the American wine-snob he was clobbering, not wine-writer's jargon in general. The look on the host's face is a little too earnestly pop-eyed in its persuasiveness: he has obviously been caught by unexpected guests without a drop of "imported wine" in his cellar; his wife is backing him loyally with a little smirk of her own that hints at hopes entertained against hope, but the male guest is clearly alarmed, and the look on *his* wife's face is one of petrifying disapproval. Nobody is harder on American wines than the Americans.

Tell your American host that you would like some characteristic dish – clam chowder, Southern fried chicken or Kansas City steak – and he will be pleased and flattered. Go on to say that you would like to accompany it with a red wine from the Napa Valley or a Hallcrest riesling, and he will protest firmly that there is plenty of Lafite or Berncasteler Doktor, and that he would not dream of offering "domestic" wine to a guest.

That, mind you is at the hands of sophisticated New Yorkers in such restaurants as Le Pavillon, hailed by the late M. Point of Vienne and M. Dumaine of Saulieu, the two greatest *restaurateurs* of our time, as the finest French restaurant outside France, or clubs such as the Racquet and Tennis or the Knickerbocker, where the wine lists do, indeed, include the finest that France and Germany can offer.

Indeed, when I last enjoyed temporary membership of the Racquet and Tennis Club which, being a sort of Park Avenue White's, is beyond my purse and above my station, there were seven clarets on the wine list of which only one, and that no more modest a wine than the 1957 Pontet Canet, was not a first growth of the Médoc, St Emilion or Pomerol, and the hocks and burgundies were of similar importance. The two "domestic" wines, a red and a white, were sold only by the carafe or the glass and not by the bottle, although they were a white pinot and a pinot noir, both from the very well-run Napa Valley vineyards, and both nominated in his book as "outstanding" by Frank Schoonmaker, the expert on French and German, as well as on Californian wines.

It may be disappointing, in such surroundings, not to be able even to buy the wine of the country, but the consolation is considerable. What is far worse is to be taken, as I have been, to some such very cheap Greenwich Village Italian restaurant as Fellin's Bocce and have my far from pecunious hosts – in this particular instance a music student and a struggling writer – vigorously resist my request for the Californian red and eventually yield only so far as I was concerned, and drink imported Bardolino themselves. Yet the American wine was exactly right with the spaghetti and meat balls, had almost certainly been far more carefully grown, shipped and bottled than the imported Italian wine, and cost only two-thirds as much.

And it was typical of American lack of confidence in the very good wines of California that when Mr Khrushchev and the late President Kennedy met in Vienna in 1961 and entertained each other to luncheon in their respective embassies, the Russians offered vodka and Soviet wines, but the Americans called in the Old World to redress the balance of the New, and served French wines only – Mouton 1953 with the main course. Mr Khrushchev scored, no doubt, with his caviar, but had President Kennedy matched California against the Crimea he would still have come off the winner.

Wine has been made in California for two hundred years, from vines of European origin and largely by families from the wine-growing countries of Europe. There is no reason why they should not be "serious" wines and, indeed, the best of them are very serious indeed. I should rank California as next after France and Germany as the wine-growing region with the highest proportion of very carefully made serious wines among its total output. Wine is made in other states of the Union, too – notably in Ohio and in New York State – but from the native American vine, *Vitis labrusca*, with results not pleasing to palates conditioned by the wines of France and Germany: they have – and the Canadian wines from Ontario that I have tasted in London have to an even greater degree – that curious earthy but sweet back-taste that the French call "foxy", characteristic of wine made from the native North-American vines. (Though I must admit that when I arrive in New York I make a beeline for the excellent oyster bar in Grand Central Station, where I wash down my plate of cherrystone clams with the dry New York State white wine they sell there by the glass, and come to no harm.) It is odd that it is on the root stocks of native American vines that the "noble" vines of Europe – producing the greatest clarets and hocks and burgundies – are now grafted as a precaution against phylloxera. Native American vines are resistant to the pest, European vines are not.

But the wines of California are made from the classic vines of Europe, and the tendency now is for the more serious Californian growers to name their wines after the grapes they come from – grapes such as the riesling, which produces the greatest wines of Germany and of Alsace; the pinot noir, responsible both for red burgundies and for champagne; and the chardonnay, from which all the great white burgundies are made.

In different soils and under different suns, of course, the same grapes will produce wines of markedly different character. The gamay, for instance, which is a common grape in Burgundy, producing *vin ordinaire*, behaves much more graciously in Beaujolais. So a Californian pinot cabernet will not smell or taste or age in bottle in the same way as burgundy or claret, though it may be made with similar care and drunk with similar seriousness. For instance, I have enjoyed at the hospitable hands of a friend at the United States Embassy a gewürztraminer from the famous Buena Vista vineyards that was less fragrant and rather sweeter than an Alsatian of the same sort, but also more delicate, and a most elegant wine in its own right.

Californian wines cannot be cheap in this country: they come from as far again beyond New York as New York is from us, and the vines they come from are tended by what I suppose must be the highest-paid vineyard workers in the world. Nor does any shipper in London that I know of import them in cask, which would reduce the cost a little, though it might also mean less reliable wines. But Stowells of Chelsea, these days, do list three Californian wines at only about fifteen shillings a bottle, all grown and shipped by the firm of Paul Masson (established in California by a Burgundian more than a century ago), of which I have enjoyed the so-called "Emerald Dry", a riesling, pale in colour, and with a slight background sweetness: it would go well with one of the creamier fish dishes or, particularly, with *sole Véronique*, because of the grapes in the sauce. Of the two reds, the cabernet sauvignon is lighter than the pinot noir: both are better than merely sound, honest wines, though I thought the two bottles that I tried could have done with a little more age (Californian wines often do not carry vintage dates, as the climate is so consistent, and bottles are understood to be ready for drinking as soon as they are on sale.)

Then, too, I have been bidden in my time by Mr Ronald Avery, head of Averys of Bristol, and a notable authority on the wines of France, which he has been buying and selling for more than forty years, to discuss with him a bottle of pinot chardonnay, from the same noble grape that, grown in France, gives us champagne and the greatest white burgundies, but this one from the Beaulieu Vineyard in the Napa Valley. "It's absurd to suppose that the finest French wines aren't better than this," said my host, "but how often does one get the finest? It's a whole lot better than most run-of-the-mill French wines, isn't it?"

Indeed it was – very like a Pouilly-Fuissé, I suggested, though perhaps a bit heavier. Which was likely enough, I suppose: the same grape, but more sunshine and, possibly, a rather richer soil. Mr Avery, who has a more poetical cast of mind than I have, and a prettier turn of phrase, proposed, "a little more voluptuous" in place of my, "a bit heavier". His other guest said that if he had been told it that was a Puligny Montrachet he would not have been surprised. All three of us agreed that it was a very serious wine indeed, and I understood how it was that Mr Avery had gone out to California to sell European wines, and had come back having bought Californian – having fallen in love with this particular wine, in fact, in the cellars at Beaulieu Vineyard.

This vineyard is one of the showplaces of the Napa Valley, which is one of the world's great wine-growing regions, and delightfully pretty, with the snowy peak of Mount St Helena looking down on orange groves and vineyards, woods and streams. It was founded by a Frenchman, Georges de Latour, descendant of a long line of Bordeaux *vignerons*, and is now conducted by his daugher, herself married to a Frenchman, and who "really tries", said Mr Avery, "to produce something out of the ordinary". We could see evidence of this in the two red wines we drank from the same vineyard, a 1951 and a 1959 cabernet sauvignon, made from the great claret-producing grape of Bordeaux, the older one (this was in 1965) by far the more elegant, something like a St Emilion of a good year and a good vineyard, the younger showing something of the lack of acidity that comes from too much sun and too rich a soil. "What the French call *plat*," said our host, but he was unable to explain how it was that, if it is a general thing for these Californian reds to lack acidity, the 1951 should have lasted so well and become so well-balanced.

Lack of acidity one knows to mean lack of balance, and one expects it to mean lack of staying power, too. Perhaps the 1951 had once been like the 1959 – it should have been, for the weather is far more consistent in California than in Bordeaux, and vintages do not vary – but what it was, in that particular case, that had kept it in such good heart must have been some quality peculiar to Californian wines.

Good as the older red wine was, though, it was the white wine we went back to talking about – went back to tasting, in my case, for there was still some in my glass, and it had held its bouquet and its flavour throughout the long meal, and had not become mawkish as it lost its first coolness. I had drunk French wines at half as much again – this would have cost rather less than a pound – that were only half as good, some of them bearing famous names. And to think that throughout my formative years "Californian" on a label meant Syrup of Figs in the bottle! I certainly would not be ashamed to offer Californian wines of this quality at my table – perhaps especially to those rich globe-trotting visitors from New York, who never seem to get them at home.

Meanwhile, though, whereas the annual consumption of wine per head in Britain is about three-and-a-half bottles, in the United States it is seven; whereas a high proportion of the British total consists of so-called "British wine" (not the genuine product of such real vineyards as Sir Guy Salisbury-Jones's at Hambledon, but factory-made from imported concentrated must, or pulp), what a vast number of American working folk drink – especially those of Greek or Italian or Latin-American origin – is the wholesome Californian wine I mention, and that whereas the more sophisticated leaders of fashion in these matters may be remiss, as I have suggested, in disregarding the best that California can offer, they are learning to appreciate the finest French and German wines in the best way of all – by drinking them.

Thus it is that some of the most scholarly writing about wines – European wines – now comes from the United States: Frank Schoonmaker is one of the great authorities on German wines; Alexis Lichine, owner of two Bordeaux châteaux and a domaine in Burgundy, with American partners and an American shipping business, is the author of the admirable *Wines of France*; and two oenologists of the University of California, Professor Amerine and Dr Singleton, won our own Wine and Food Society's André Simon award in 1966 with their book, *Wine*, for the year's best contribution to the literature of gastronomy.

For centuries now, London has been the wine capital of the world: its wine trade is experienced and scholarly, and the British middle classes have up till now had the money to indulge a cultivated taste. But ever since the middle nineteen-fifties (the great 1956 frosts in the Bordelais were really the turning point) the price of the finest wines has been going up, so that less and less of it is coming here, and more and more to the United States: in 1961 when Lafite fetched the highest price ever recorded for a French red wine on first being offered, how many old-established independent London wine-merchants failed, for the first time, to buy any of the first growths of a great year? And where did most of the first growths go to?

Instead, we are getting to know the *bourgeois* clarets and the lesser-known wines of France, to say nothing of the wines of Yugoslavia, Chile, Turkey, the Soviet Union and other places that before the war we had never heard of, or at any rate never thought of, as wine-growers. The *bourgeois* growths of Bordeaux are very good, and those that come to this country are carefully picked by shippers and merchants that really know about claret. But wine scholarship has to be refreshed by occasional reminders of what the finest wines smell and look and taste like, just as theatre critics must occasionally be reminded, by a Gielgud in *Hamlet*, say, of the standards set by great artists and great poets. So I foresee a time when, although Britain will still be noted among amateurs of wine for the range and variety of its lists, drawing upon every wine country in the world for good and interesting wines, it will be the United States, looking no farther than its own frontiers – except perhaps to such neighbours as Chile – for the cheaper wines, that will have learned to appreciate, by being able to afford, the finest clarets and the greatest hocks, and New York, not London, will be the capital of wine scholarship.

"The grand object of travelling is to see the shores of the Mediterranean," observed Dr Johnson, and I have drunk respectable wines on pretty well all of its shores, though I would not include among them the deep pink and heavily scented contents of a bottle served to me at a picnic by the Dead Sea, labelled "*Hock d'Origine: Produce of Bethlehem*". But when I opened the first article on wine that I ever wrote for *The Times*, a dozen years ago, by stating that virtually wherever the Roman soldier trod, save only in Britain, grew and still grows the vine, and a distinguished classical scholar and writer on wine objected, "except, also, in Egypt," I was able to reply that my critic had clearly not enjoyed at Shepheard's Hotel in Cairo, as I had – if enjoyed is precisely the word I am looking for – a bottle of "Clos des Pyramides".

Another Jordanian wine that came my way in those parts, besides the Bethlehem hock, when in 1958 I again found myself a correspondent with British troops, was Latroun, which occasioned some soldierly jests; I have been served a good red local wine by Polish nuns in what was then the Jordanian sector of Jerusalem; and a Lebanese white wine from the hills above Beirut has washed down for me a giant of a local *langouste*.

I have heard tell of a British diplomatist who, having been ambassador in Athens, was promoted to Paris, where he used to have retsina shipped to him by the case from Greece, as the only wine worth drinking, thus confirming his French friends in their belief that the British are barbarians, anyway. I do not think I am ever likely to get into that lamentable state: I can drink retsina twice a day in Greece for weeks, and then forget about it for the next five years. In any case, there are many more unresinated wines available in Greece than there used to be – thanks, I suppose, to demands by tourists – and I think that even the Greeks themselves are drinking less retsina as a result. All the same, there have been occasions at, for instance, the White Tower restaurant in Percy Street, with the fiercely bewhiskered faces of the Byronic heroes of the War of Independence glowering down upon me from the prints upon the wall, when it has been agreeable to be re-minded, on a grey London day, by the resinated wine of Attica, that somewhere there is a wine-dark sea, and a violet light over Hymettus, and that the klephts who carved the Turks of the eighteen-twenties into particularly small pieces did so with the taste of turpentine in their mouths.

The best retsina comes from the middle of Attica (northern Greece produces fine, full red wines, unresinated), and such a place as Marcopoulo, a mere twenty miles from Athens, is one of the many little towns that live entirely by the grape: all its six or seven thousand inhabitants are concerned in one way or another, full-time or part-time, directly or indirectly, with growing or pressing or bottling or coopering. Five hundred of its eight hundred houses have each their little wooden presses, though I have seen the local doctor's crop being pressed in the oldest way of all, trodden by the feet of three of his neighbours. There is also a co-operative with French and Italian machinery, which exports a good deal of retsina to the United States, where not only Greek-Americans but Italo-Americans have a taste for it.

To make the local white wine into retsina, lumps of resin from the local pine-trees, milk-white and tacky to the finger, are added during fermentation, and the retsina one drinks in the local *tavernas* is always the wine of the year: more than a year old, the head of the co-operative told me, and the wine takes on a musty taste, which seems to disprove the theory that the origin of retsina is that the ancient Greeks used resin as a preservative.

"Much more likely", someone suggested, "to take away the taste of the goatskins it was carried in." And, "Rather taste the goatskins", observed an as yet unconverted English visitor. Whatever the reason for resinating wine, there is no doubt about the long history of the practice in these parts, and another odd survival is the adding of salt, which is still done in some of the small wineries there for special customers who insist on it. The ancient Greeks used to dilute their wine with sea-water, and took the custom to Magna Graecia, which is how the Romans came to write about it; and still, in the heart of Attica, you can take your wine with a pinch of salt, yet know the story to be true.

Every night, throughout September, there is a wine festival in a natural park at the very edge of Athens, by the little monastery of Daphni, floodlit for the occasion. For fifteen drachmas at the gate, which is about three-and-sixpence, you pick up your jug and your glass and go around the booth where the barrels are stacked high, and the girls, in their regional rig-outs, will give you a taste in your glass before you decide on a jugful. Or you can have a jugful of everything – as much as a gullet will swallow and a belly will hold, for your fifteen drachmas, if gullet and belly begin at seven o'clock and go on until midnight.

At the last Daphni festival I went to, there were seventy-four wines to choose from – white wines, red wines, and pink wines; dry wines and sweet wines; wines from Crete and Rhodes, Samos and Patmos, Mytilene and Cos and Cephalonia; mainland and island. But why do I say, to choose from?

– there is nothing, save the march of time, to prevent your trying them all, and there were sturdy Greeks there, with mountainous wives, who were doing their damnedest to make it.

For this still remains more of a local jollification than an entertainment specially contrived for tourists, though that I suppose is what it will become. But as recently as 1965 I was told – and hardly needed to be told: one could see – that the five thousand visitors a night were mostly Athenians: families with picnic baskets, babies and grandmas, pretty girls in summer frocks and hairy girls with sweat stains under their arms; plump middle-aged couples and naval cadets in white drill with dirks at their hips; and a few wondering foreigners such as us, not to mention an Italian tripper we had fallen in with, who was only just drunk enough, he told us, to think it funny to pretend to be drunk, and who kept breaking into the more hackneyed arias from the better-known operas, proving once again that it is untrue that the Italians love music: they love Italian music.

Not that anyone was really drunk, or even mildly tiddly. Imagine such a place in England, either outrageously expensive, to keep the yobs out, and desperately class- or at any rate money-conscious, or else cheap and full of drunks, littered with broken bottles, and copulating couples under every tree. The wine festival at Daphni is more like Copenhagen's Tivoli Gardens, for all the difference of race and climate and what there is to drink, in being a place where all classes are at their ease, and enjoy themselves without making asses of themselves.

There are cheap snack-bars, with savoury hot meat-balls, spicy stuffed vine-leaves, and the nut-and-honey sweetmeats that the Greeks love, and either taught the Turks about or learned from the Turks, according to your view of the origins of the Greek cuisine. There is a self-service restaurant, where the baby lamb roasting on a spit scents the air, and a *de luxe* open-air restaurant where you have the best view of the evening's folk-dancing, with the high-booted and heavily moustachioed Cretans leaping and twirling, the dark-eyed Macedonian girls all a-jingle with their bracelets and their necklets, and there are seats and tables for those who have brought their own vast suppers – the Greeks are heroic eaters.

I arrived late, began with retsina, and then tasted a dry white wine from Samos. I was urged to a red wine from Crete, crisp to the tongue, and fragrant to the nose, and the Italian broke off in the middle of something from *Cavalleria Rusticana* to ply me with what he declared to have found, after unusually extensive researches, to be the best retsina at the festival. I had dined already, and had had my ouzo at Floca's, watching the smart Athenian world go by, and dry, white Pallini Alpha with fried mussels from Salonika at the Dionysos restaurant by the Acropolis, with the floodlit Parthenon afloat in a blue velvet sky. So I had room now only for something blander and softer to finish the evening with, and a pretty girl wearing a pillbox hat with a gold tassel, the national dress of who knows what remote and mountainous corner of Greece, drew Mavrodaphne for me from the barrel – sweet, full, and rich with the scent of muscat grapes. It was eleven o'clock now, when the serving finishes (you can go on drinking what is in your jug until midnight) and I had tasted only five wines out of seventy-four: what a pity I thought, that the festival's only rule is that you must not carry any wine away from it except in your own skin.

There is tolerable red wine to be had in Libya, grown in the vineyards established there by Mussolini's Italian settlers, and very sound red wines indeed now come to Britain from Tunisia and Morocco. But the biggest and most advanced of the wine-growing countries of North Africa is Algeria – indeed, after Italy, France and Spain, the fourth biggest in the world – and I have tried to find out why its red wines, always cheap and often very good, are still under such a cloud in this country.

It seems that after the fall of France, many French ships on the high seas carrying wine from Algiers to France and other overseas markets put into British ports, and by December 1940 there was lying in our dock warehouses a hundred times as much Algerian wine as Britain had imported per year before the war.

What to do with a hundred years' supply of Algerian wine? H.M. Customs, whose problem it was, insisted that it be labelled "Produce of North Africa" or "Produce of Algeria", but it all went like hot cakes, and there were no complaints, whether from customers or suppliers, during the otherwise lean years of 1940 to 1944. My old friend, Dr Fritz Hallgarten, head of the firm of London wine-shippers, who was consulted at the time, tells me that the red wines were very good – "very high alcoholic strength, enormous body and flavour" – probably ordered by French exporters to blend with the inferior wines of the Midi. The white wines were disappointing, having oxidized in the warehouses, but were sold to make vermouth – quite successfully.

It was after the war that the trouble arose. British experts went to Algiers after it had been liberated, but before France was completely free, to select wines that would be part of a barter deal between British and French governments, and again the first shipments were welcomed everywhere. But when France itself was freed, many shippers preferred to wait until it was possible again to import clarets and burgundies and did not take up their quotas of Algerian, which lay in the warehouses, deteriorating in cask, because of lack of skilled attention in the way of topping up and sulphuring, long after they should have been bottled.

Now whether it was – as some allege, but I do not want to scratch at old sores – that one or two interested firms began a whispering campaign against the Algerian wine, or that some of the spoiled wine did reach the British market and disappoint post-war wine-drinkers, who now had good French wine from which to draw comparisons, I do not know. (It is interesting, by the way, that most of this spoiled wine was eventually sold to defeated Germany.) What does seem certain is that quite a lot of Algerian wine was drunk and enjoyed in this country until twenty years ago, and that its unfortunate reputation dates from no longer ago than that.

As the late Allan Sichel wrote, in his *Penguin Book on Wines*, they should be taken on their merits these days, "and old prejudices forgotten". He had found, incidentally, that some that arrived in 1943, as ballast in returning transports, was very good indeed, "the best of which proved capable of great improvement in bottle and made good drinking in 1958 or 1959". Poor wine cannot improve in bottle over such a long period.

I know that there are stricter Muslim states, such as Pakistan, but in the Mediterranean Arab countries, the religious ban on making and drinking wine is generally regarded as being out of date: in Tunis, for instance, the French and Italian wine-growers have now been expropriated and the vineyards are in Tunisian hands. A senior government official there told me that he reckoned that the current view of 85 per cent or more of the population was that the Prophet was not against wine, but merely against its abuse. This relaxed attitude, together with the growing tourist trade, and the consequent accelerated westernization of the Tunisians of the cities and the resorts, is encouraging greater and more varied wine-growing. Similar influences are at work in Algeria, Morocco and, to a lesser extent, Libya, and will have a considerable effect on production for export as well as for the home markets.

In Israel, curiously enough, where Judaism does not at all forbid wine – indeed, wine is a part of all religious festivals, particularly the Passover – very little is drunk, except on such occasions, though some very respectable wine is grown. A high proportion of the tourists, so far, are American Jews, not themselves wine-drinkers, and it was sometimes as much as I could do in Israel, even in an expensive restaurant, to get a wine list: I was expected to make do with iced water and coffee, like other English-speaking patrons.

Here, it is the latest and poorest immigrants who have a tradition of wine-drinking – the "Oriental" Jews (so-called, though many of them come from the farthest west of the Mediterranean) were used to drinking cheap local wine in Morocco and Algeria, and the wineries of Israel are producing increasing amounts of drinkable cheap *vin ordinaire* for them. Unfortunately, these are not the people who set the patterns of social behaviour for Jerusalem, Haifa and Tel Aviv, or the restaurants there might put it on their table as carafe wine, and the more sophisticated Israelis of European origin take to it, too, stimulating further production and lower prices.

It is Jews, oddly enough, and Russian refugees who grow wine in Iran, where they seem sterner about these things than their fellow-Muslims of the Arab countries, perhaps because they are of a different sect. Quite an amount of drink gets put away by the locals, and not only wine but hard liquor such as arrack and the local vodka (some of the best caviar in the world comes from these parts, so why not vodka?) But the general tone is more puritanical here, and one modest hotel I stayed at had to send out for wine and brandy for me, and very nasty they were.

I do not know how true it is that

> ... *the Lion and the Lizard keep*
> *The Courts where Jamshyd gloried and drank deep*

but at the top, or smarter, end of Tehran, where the Shahan-shah himself recently declared the new Hilton Hotel open (I think he has some money in it), there is a supermarket and a Miami nightclub, one restaurant called Barbecue and another called The Hot Shoppe.

Down in the centre of the city, too, where the red double-decker buses ply, the bazaar will have to exoticize itself some-what if the tourists from the Hilton are going to be able to boast back home of what they picked up there, In a Persian Market, for a song. When I strolled among the stalls offering plastic-handled, nylon-bristled toothbrushes; cotton rugs from India featuring dear little pussies; Kleenex; Carr's bis-cuits and genuine Texas jeans; virtually the only echo from the Arabian Nights that reached my wistful ear was the trade-mark on the paraffin stoves for sale: Aladdin.

Yet only an hour by air from the tall tower that is the Hilton are the domes and minarets of Isfahan – once, to the marvelling eyes of Elizabethan Englishmen, the most splendid capital in the world, and still distilling a magic compounded partly of blue-and-gold tiles reflected in ornamental water, partly of the crowded clamour of the vast bazaar and the bustle of the streets.

All the same, and even in the gardens of Isfahan, I was thinking of a remoter garden still, and a voice farther away in time than those proclaiming in organized and amplified spontaneity their enthusiasm for the Government's latest measure of land reform: how could I visit Persia without making pilgrimage to the tomb of old Khayyam?

And so I took the Golden Road to Samarkand – those six hundred miles of it, at any rate, that run from Tehran almost to the Soviet frontier; and I took them the easiest way: two hours by air to Meshed, and another couple by road, back on my tracks to Naishapur, rather than spend twenty-four hours in the train, or a couple of days in a car.

The desert and the mountains, which press closely in on Meshed, press closer still on Naishapur. But at the edge of the little town, after a dusty jolting over seventy miles of made but unsurfaced road, we suddenly turned off over smooth tarmac, skirting as primitive a mud village as any you would see in Afghanistan – not all that far from Meshed – and great gates set in brave new brick opened on to the blue-domed shrine of the holy man, Muhammed Mahruq, in the garden of which Omar lies buried.

Even the tarmac, with its sodium-vapour lamps, the new wall and the fancy gates, had not prepared me. Over-topping and outfacing all is a modernistic, latticed, elongated dome, more than sixty feet high, of concrete and coloured tiles, fenced in by massive cones of concrete that would look like a tank trap if it were not for the floodlights set in them.

My interpreter gestured grandly, and I protested, "No, no: there must be some mistake! Omar's is a *little* tomb, close to the wall of the shrine. . . ." And I added, lamely, that I had read as much, for I had never set foot in Naishapur before, though I could have cried out loud that Omar *couldn't* lie under this gimmicky erection from a World's Fair. Not Omar. Not at rest.

Alas, there was no mistake. We walked under the tall lamp standards that line the path to the tomb, all aluminium paint and cubist panes of glass, while the cooing doves deposited their own art criticisms on the top of the new memorial, and my interpreter explained.

It had been finished only a month or so, he said, but the local unco' guid had long been agitating for the move: the shrine was a holy man's, whereas Omar had been a drinking man, and not fit to lie so close – hence the removal of his remains 100 yards or so from the wall of the shrine. It was like keeping a decent distance between Robert Burns's remains and those of John Knox.

"After all," the boy went on, at the look on my face, "we *are* Muslims, and Meshed and Naishapur are places of pilgrimage."

"So you don't drink wine," I said, "in Naishapur and Meshed?" – knowing well that there were vineyards hard by, and that I had drunk good Iranian wine in Tehran and Isfahan, and perfectly horrible Iranian wine in Meshed, to say nothing of Iranian Grande Champagne Cognac Impériale, made by a company called Ararat, and smelling of chocolate creams.

"Oh, yes," he said, "and especially on Saturday nights. But even those who do, don't expect to lay their bones by a holy man's, and they don't think Omar should, either."

We had reached the wall of the shrine, where the tomb used to be, "And *you actually moved his bones*", I cried, "from here to there!" Not, I was told, until they had been sent first to Tehran to be, as my interpreter put it, "analysed". And by this time he must have been enjoying my incredulous disapproval, for he added, gratuitously, that the modest white memorial stone, too small to be appropriately accommodated under the vast new monument, had been moved to a square in the town – just by the Khayyam Cinema.

It was another poet, under later and greyer skies, who pleaded:

Good frend for Jesus sake forbeare,
To digg the dust encloased heare.
Blest be ye man yt spares thes stones.
And curst be he yt moves my bones.

and, in spite of all temptations, and letters to *The Times*, we have dutifully forborne. Poor Omar, though, less lucky in his countrymen, prophesied all too truly, eight centuries ago:

Ah, Moon of my delight who know'st no wane,
The Moon of Heav'n is rising once again:
How oft hereafter rising shall she look
Through this same Garden after me – in vain!

Back in Meshed, the British Council man said that he didn't believe it was because Omar was a drinking man: the Iranians had just got around to his being a tourist attraction, and the removal of his bones was only incidental to tarting up the tomb. In Tehran, a man from the Ministry of Propaganda said yes, they *had* wanted to give Omar a more resplendent memorial, to please the visitors, but it was true, too, that it wouldn't have pleased the pious if it had been too near the holy man's.

Whatever the reason, I reached for my Iranian Grande Champagne Cognac Impériale, drank deep and, mindful of the old gentleman's last words, turned down an empty glass.

I I · *Afterthoughts on Mornings After*

The poignant lines were scribbled on the back of an envelope
that had been slipped between the pages of a second-hand
copy I had picked up somewhere of Saintsbury's *Notes on a
Cellar Book*:

> *It is no time for mirth and laughter,*
> *The cold grey dawn of the morning after –*

and for a long time I did not know and could not trace the
author, but quoting them in *The Observer* brought a letter
from Mr Peter Hunt, anthologist of eating and drinking, who
referred me to the work of George Ade, one of those great

Chicago newspapermen of just before and just after the First
World War, and a chronicler of the old pre-Volstead saloons.*
Sure enough, I discovered a song from his musical comedy,
The Sultan of Sulu, the chorus of which runs:

> *R – E – M – O – R – S – E*
> *The water wagon is the place for me;*
> *At twelve o'clock I felt immense,*
> *Today I favour total abstinence,*
> *My eyes are bleared and red and hot,*
> *I ought to eat but I cannot,*
> *It is no time for mirth and laughter,*
> *The cold grey dawn of the morning after.*

For those in so sad a condition, when the Remembrance of
Things Past follows one around like a personal black thunder-
cloud, Byron would have prescribed a hock-and-seltzer,
which I have always found a rather mawkish mixture: other
gentlemen of the period simply scraped the fur from their
matutinal tongues with those instruments of silver on turned
ivory handles that are still occasionally to be bought from
dealers in Georgian silver, and known simply as tongue-
scrapers. In the hock country itself they take raw herring,
onions and sour cream on the morning after, a specific much
too heroic for me. Nor do I take any more kindly to Mr
Raymond Postgate's glass of cold milk on going to bed and
another on rising: I am not a calf. There are those, nowadays,
who swear by a hair of the dog, and who breakfast on Bass
and aspirin. Some will have nothing but champagne; others
speak highly, if in a hoarse voice, of absinthe.

This must all be based on some sort of sympathetic magic,
on the principle of strong devils driving out weaker devils,

* Last year, 1966, was the centenary of his birth. *The Sultan of Sulu* was first
produced in 1902.

and I have my doubts about it, as does the American, Mr David Embury, author of *The Fine Art of Mixing Drinks*, who points out that, "you don't treat arsenic poisoning by taking more arsenic, or ptomaine poisoning by eating more contaminated food. Why be so naïve as to imagine that you can cure alcohol poisoning by drinking more alcohol?" Though I have known a Horse's Neck, which is brandy and ginger-ale, bring round a sorely afflicted destroyer captain to the belief that he would live, and his ship float. And then there are those who prescribe various patent bitters, such as Fernet Branca and Underberg, presumably on that other well-known principle that anything that tastes nasty must be doing you good.

Among the ancient remedies collected by Mr Hunt, who tracked down my George Ade quotation for me, are Brillat-Savarin's, "a good pint of chocolate mixed with amber in the proportion of from sixty to seventy grains to the pound"; the recipe of the seventeenth-century scientist, Robert Boyle, for an, "after-drinking cure for the heid-ake: Take green Hemlock that is tender, and put it in your Socks, so that it may lie thinly between them and the Soles of your Feet: shift the Herbs once a Day"; and an eighteenth-century Surfeit-water that contains twenty-one different herbs and, "is used successfully against cholicks, gripings in the stomach and bowels, flatulencies and vapours, all of which it discusses by its carminative virtue; it attentuates the humours, and helps perspiration, and is therefore good in all epidemical and contagious distempers. It resists putrefaction and expels the malignity from the centre to the circumference, which it discharges by a gentle dew upon the surface of the cuticle."

This is to sweat it out, and upon the same principle a Turkish bath is many a repentant imbiber's first thought. On my first and only visit to Baden-Baden, the masseur at the thermal baths there, slapping the salient of my stomach with Teutonic playfulness and a soapy brush, inquired, "Vhisky, eh?" – this obviously being his stock conversation-opener for outlanders – and I replied, with as much hauteur as a man may muster who is lying naked on his back, having his stomach slapped by a foreigner to whom he has not been properly introduced: "Not at all; it's Schwarzwaldischer kirschwasser," thus not only exhausting the greater part of my stock of restaurant German, but paying a well-deserved tribute to a potent local tipple. The first course at dinner the previous evening had been paper-thin slices of Black Forest smoked ham, accompanied by the strong, dry, colourless schnapps distilled from the local cherries, and we had gone back to the same *kirschwasser*, perhaps unwisely, with our coffee after dinner: the memory remained with me as I spent my morning at the Baden-Baden baths, being boiled in the service of my paper, for which I was writing a travel article.

No doubt by the same open-the-pores principle a really hot curry would do – for anyone who can face curry for breakfast on a hungover morning – and opening the pores may be the reason, too, for all these various pick-me-ups based on Worcester sauce. Mr Anthony Burgess has written somewhere that Evelyn Waugh advocated a lump of sugar, soaked in Angostura and rolled in red pepper, placed in a glass of champagne, so that each bubble bore a grain of pepper to the palate, "painfully delicious". (Not that Mr Burgess should need such specifics: he claims of his favourite tonic, Hangman's Blood, not only that it tastes very smooth, and induces a somehow metaphysical elation, but that it rarely leaves a hangover. Which is quite remarkable, seeing that it consists of a double each of gin, whisky, rum, port and brandy poured into a pint glass, to which a small bottle of stout is added, the whole lot being topped up with champagne. Mr Burgess does not say so, but I think that this is meant for more than one.)

Fresh air, on the other hand, is declared by an American professor, in a paper read to the American Association for the Advancement of Science (what worth-while subjects for discussion the Association chooses!) to be no better than any other sort of air; and black coffee is a stimulant, not a sedative.

My own preference is for nothing more magical or esoteric than the patent medicine, Alka-Seltzer, that admirable corrective for gluttony and alcoholic remorse. (Boots market a version of their own, called Solzets – I think they should have sought a more memorable name). Take no notice of the namby-pamby instructions on the bottle about one or two tablets' being the adult dose, but put four in a tumbler of water, the colder the better – a lump of ice does not come amiss – and let any genteel inhibitions about belching go with the wind. But I cock a wary eye at those hardened sinners who lace the Alka-Seltzer with a large gin. True, I have seen a chemist's writing somewhere that it is ridiculous to suppose that anything will cure a hangover, and that the effect of effervescent alkalis is purely psychological. So, very often, is a hangover: if I should seem to have a hangover, I should be quite pleased to have it seem to be cured.

There is something to be said, too, for a very long, very cold glass of one of the plain, unsweetened and unfermented apple-juices, either Bulmer's Applejoy or Shloer – to my mind, the best of all non-alcoholic drinks in any circumstances, especially with food, and particularly good after over-indulgence, being cleansing to the palate and, as it is rather laxative and diuretic, to other parts, too.

I have read somewhere that in the New York of the eighteen-nineties habitual drunkards were bled by the application of specially selected leeches: creatures that are said to be normally teetotal, but which occasionally become addicted to drink, taken through the patient's blood, which they suck – much to the patient's relief – until they themselves fall stupefied to the ground. Two pounds of honey and twenty-four hours of rest constitute a gentler specific, recommended in an amusing little book on the folklore of restoratives, *A Cordiall Water*, by that scholarly American gastronome, Mrs M. F. K. Fisher, which contains another recipe involving honey that is said not only to cure a hangover but also to remove all further desire for strong drink – a pity, it seems to me. It is called Dr Jarvis's Honey Cure, and calls for the consumption of eighteen teaspoons of honey, six at a time, at twenty-minute intervals, repeated in three hours. Leave a bottle of whisky by the bed, which the patient can drink from if he wants. Next morning, repeat the previous day's honey routine, follow with a boiled egg, and then in ten minutes give six more teaspoons of honey. For lunch, give four teaspoons of honey, a glass of tomato juice, a portion of chopped beef (a hamburger, or raw?) and four more teaspoons of honey. Leave the bottle of whisky on the table and, says Dr Jarvis, "it will probably not be drunk".

And then, of course, there is the most famous hangover cure of all, the Prairie Oyster, which is the raw yolk of an egg slipped unbroken into a glass containing a tablespoon of Worcester sauce, with a dash of sherry and a touch of red pepper. To my mind, anyone who can even think of the raw yolk of an egg cannot really be hungover.

There are those, though, who take it – the whole raw egg, indeed – every morning of their lives. I was once relaxing after a hearty Irish breakfast at the Shelbourne Hotel in Dublin, when into the lounge walked a bright yellow suit with a loud black overcheck, a double-breasted waistcoat, jewelled tiepin, heavy watch-chain, yellow carnation and, inside it all, a chubby American gentleman who proceeded to give an order to the waiter that made me doubt the evidence of my ears. The waiter disappeared to return with two tall glasses on a tray, each filled with a viscous-seeming liquid the colour of uncooked brains. The waiter told me later that yes, I *had* heard aright: there was one raw egg in each glass, beaten up into a glass of port and a glass of brandy. And, having vouchsafed this information, he then hurried off to fetch the third glass of the same that the chubby American gentleman was urgently signalling for.

The following morning (wearing a bright green blazer, a fancy waistcoat with contrasting lapels and pocket-flaps, and a white carnation), the chubby Amercian gentleman was clearly concerned not to have to waste his time over sending for second helpings: the initial order was for three, not two, tall glasses of the mixture, and yet, even so, there came peremptory signals for a fourth. The waiter confided in me later that in his opinion the customary breakfast – if I may so describe it – had got off to a rather late start, and the chubby American gentleman had decided to carry on with the same rather than switch over at eleven, as was his wont, to his usual mid-morning snack of double Tio Pepes.

Between the two breakfasts, I had seen him at Jammet's, preparing the way for dinner with champagne cocktails – this time he was in pale grey, with a pink carnation – and on each of the three occasions he carried a different walking-stick. Each stick, according to the waiter at the Shelbourne, contained a long thin flask of Irish whiskey.

It was a few days later, on the other side of Ireland, at my hotel in Galway, that I actually made the acquaintance of this flamboyant character. I had been deeply interested, I told him, in his Dublin breakfasts.

He nodded weightily and said, *"Better than cornflakes."*

Was I right, I asked, in understanding that the proportions were quite simple – one egg, one port, one brandy? Quite right, said the chubby American gentleman: quite right.

And then he flushed deeply, his voice rose, his hand shook: there were those, he exclaimed – I would hardly believe it, but there were those who put sugar in the mixture, and nutmeg on the top: "Junk!" he cried: "JUNK!"

I digress, though, from hangovers, the real answer to which, of course, is prevention rather than cure, and it is said that almonds, or oil, or milk, taken before a party or a dinner, will delay and diminish the effects of too much alcohol. Some say that one should stick either to grain or to grape, others that one should not mix drinks at all – not even wine with brandy.

In what seems to be a learned book, *A Man May Drink*, written by a pseudonymous consultant surgeon, the theory is propounded that it is the congenerics – those substances other than alcohol from which beverages derive their various flavours, scents and characters – that give rise to headaches and other toxic effects. A chart gives the proportion of congenerics to alcohol in various drinks, and is held by the author to prove that hangover symptoms are most likely to occur with the very best whiskies, and least likely with vodka and gin, but that in view of "the insidious nature of the neutral spirits", beer is best.

May be, may be. Myself, I would rather drink claret with my dinner, and take the consequences. The difficulty is that all too often a heavy head on, say, Boxing Day morning is as much the result of too much food, too much noise, and too much tobacco smoke, as of too much wine. But it is not a bad idea at a heavy dinner-party to serve cold table waters – Vichy or Perrier: I prefer the fizzy Perrier myself – as well as wine. Quench your thirst with the water, and take it turn about with the wine: it not only reduces the wine intake, but corrects acidity, and freshens the palate for each course and each bottle. This is one of the more civilized French and Italian table habits, and I wish it were more usual here. So does many a liver of my acquaintance.

Index

189